FORGET FOUCAULT
Jean Baudrillard

&
FORGET BAUDRILLARD
An Interview with Sylvère Lotringer

SEMIOTEXT(E) FOREIGN AGENTS SERIES

"Forget Baudrillard" is first published in this
volume. "Forget Foucault" was originally published in 1977 as *Oublier Foucault*, Paris Editions
Galileé. This translation first appeared as "Forgetting Foucault" in *Humanities in Society*, Volume 3,
Number 1, and is reprinted by permission of the
publisher.

Special thanks to Phil Beitchman, Nicole
Dufresne, Ronald Gottesman, Lee Hildreth,
Lewanne Jones, Christopher Mays, Mark Polizzotti,
and Christoph Cox.

Semiotext(e)
522 Philosophy Hall
Columbia University
New York, NY 10027

Contents

Forget Foucault 7
Forget Baudrillard 65

Forget Foucault

Forget Foucault

Foucault's writing is perfect in that the very movement of the text gives an admirable account of what it proposes: on one hand, a powerful generating spiral that is no longer a despotic architecture but a filiation *en abyme*, coil and strophe without origin (without catastrophe, either), unfolding ever more widely and rigorously; but on the other hand, an interstitial flowing of power that seeps through the whole porous network of the social, the mental, and of bodies, infinitesimally modulating the technologies of power (where the relations of power and seduction are inextricably entangled). All this reads *directly* in Foucault's discourse (which is *also* a discourse of power). It flows, it invests and saturates, the entire space it opens. The smallest qualifiers find their way into the slightest interstices of meaning; clauses and chapters wind into spirals; a magistral art of decentering allows the opening of new spaces (spaces of power and of discourse) which are immediately covered up by the meticulous outpouring of Foucault's writing. There's no vacuum here, no phantasm, no backfiring, but a fluid objectivity, a nonlinear, orbital, and flawless writing. The meaning never exceeds what one says of it; no dizziness, yet it never floats in a text too big for it: no rhetoric either.

In short, Foucault's discourse is a mirror of the powers it describes. It is there that its strength and its seduction lie, and not at all in its "truth index," which is only its leitmotiv: these procedures of truth are of no importance, for Foucault's discourse is no truer than any other. No, its strength and its seduction are in the analysis which unwinds the subtle meanderings of its object, describing it with a tactile and tactical exactness, where seduction feeds analytical force and where language itself gives birth to the operation of new powers. Such also is the operation of myth, right down to the symbolic effectiveness described by Lévi-Strauss. Foucault's is not therefore a discourse of truth but a mythic discourse in the strong sense of the word, and I secretly believe that it has no illusions about the effect of truth it produces. That, by the way, is what is missing in those who follow in Foucault's footsteps and pass right by this mythic arrangement to end up with the truth, nothing but the truth.

The very perfection of this analytical chronicle of power is disturbing. Something tells us — but implicitly, as if seen in a reverse shot of this writing too beautiful to be true — that if it is possible at last to talk with such definitive understanding about power, sexuality, the body, and discipline, even down to their most delicate metamorphoses, it is because at some point *all this is here and now over with*. And because Foucault can only draw such an admirable picture since he works at the confines of an area (maybe a "classical age," of which he would be the last great dinosaur) now in the process of collapsing entirely. Such a configuration lends itself to the most dazzling display of analysis just before its terms have been recalled. "When I speak of time, that's because it's already no longer there," said Apollinaire. But what if Foucault spoke so well to us concerning power — and let us not forget it, in *real* objective terms which cover manifold diffractions but nonetheless do not question the objective point of view one has about them, and concerning power which is pulverized but whose *reality principle* is nonetheless not questioned — only because power is dead? Not merely impossible to locate because of dissemination, but dissolved purely and simply in a manner that still escapes us, dissolved by reversal, cancellation, or made hyper-real through simulation (who knows?). Nonetheless, something happened at the level of power which Foucault cannot grasp once again from deep within his genealogy: for him the political has no end, but only metamorphoses from the "despotic" to the "disciplinary," and at this level to the "microcellular," according to the same process belonging to the physical and biological sciences. This may constitute enormous progress over the imaginary order of power which dominates us — but nothing has changed concerning the *axiom* of power: it doesn't exceed its shadow, i.e., the smallest definition of its *real* function. Power, then, is still turned toward a reality principle and a very strong truth principle; it is still oriented toward a possible coherence of politics and discourse (power no longer pertains to the despotic order of what is forbidden and of the law, but it still belongs to the objective order of the real). Foucault can thus describe to us the successive spirals of power, the last of which enables him to mark its most minute terminations, although power never ceases being the term, and the question of its extermination can never arise.

And what if Foucault spoke to us so well of sexuality (at last an *analytical* discourse on sex — or a discourse freed from the pathos of sex — that has the textual clarity of discourses which *precede the discovery of the unconscious* and which do not need the "blackmail of the deep" to say what they have to say), what if he spoke so well of sexuality only because its form, this great *production* (that too) of our culture, was, like that of power, in the process of disappearing? Sex, like man, or like the category of the social, may only last for a while. And what if sex's reality effect, which is at the horizon of the discourse on sexuality, also started to fade away radically, giving way to other simulacra and dragging down with it the great referents of desire, the body, and the unconscious — that whole recitative which is so powerful today? Foucault's hypothesis itself suggests how mortal sex is sooner or later. While psychoanalysis seemingly inaugurates the millenium of sex and desire, it is perhaps what orchestrates it in full view before it disappears altogether. In a certain way, psychoanalysis puts an end to the unconscious and desire, just as Marxism put an end to the class struggle, because it hypostatizes them and buries them in their theoretical project. We have at this point reached the *metalanguage* of desire in a discourse on sex that has outreached itself by redoubling the signs of sex so as to mask an indeterminacy and a profound disinvestment — the dominant catchword *sexual* is now equivalent to an inert sexual milieu. It is the same with sex as with politics: "Remember in '68 how many strikes, barricades, speeches and cobblestones it took for people to begin to accept that *everything is political*. Pornography, as it proliferates and is censured only to come back stronger, will let them see that *everything is sexuality*" (*Art Press*, issue on pornography[1]). There is a double absurdity here (everything is political, everything is sexuality), a parallel absurdity in these two catchwords at the very moment when politics collapses and when sex itself becomes involuted and disappears as a strong referent in the hyperreality of "liberated" sexuality.

If, as Foucault states, the bourgeoisie used sex and sexuality to give itself a glorious body and a prestigious truth in order to pass this on then to the rest of society under the guise of truth and banal destiny, it could just be that this simulacrum slips out of its skin and departs with it. Because he remains within the classic formula of sex, Foucault cannot trace this new spiral of sexual simulation in which sex finds a second existence and takes on the fascination of a lost frame of reference* (and this is nothing but the coherence lent by a given configuration to the *myth* of the unconscious). Even if he fashions sex into a discursive configuration, this has its own internal coherence and, just like power, it has a positive index of refraction. Discourse is discourse, but the operations, strategies, and schemes played out there are real: the hysterical woman, the perverse adult, the masturbating child, the oedipal family. These real, historical devices, machines that have never been tampered with — no more so than the "desiring machines" in their order of libidinal energy — all exist, and the truth is: *they have been true.* But Foucault cannot tell us anything about the simulating machines that double each one of these "original" machines, about the great simulating mechanism which winds all these devices into a wider spiral, because Foucault's gaze is fixed upon the classic "semiurgy" of power and sex. He does not see the frenzied semiurgy that has taken hold of the simulacrum.

*It may well be that pornography is there only to reactivate this lost referent in order to prove *a contrario*, by its grotesque hyperrealism, that there is however some *real* sex somewhere.

Maybe this spiral that erases all others is only a new aspect of desire or power, but this is very unlikely because it breaks down all discourse into these terms. Barthes said of Japan: "There, sexuality is in sex and nowhere else. In the United States, sexuality is everywhere except in sex."[2] And what if sex itself is no longer in sex? We are no doubt witnessing, with sexual liberation, pornography, etc., the agony of sexual reason. And Foucault will only have given us the key to it when it no longer means anything. The same goes for *Discipline and Punish*, with its theory of discipline, of the "panoptic" and of "transparence." A magistral but obsolete theory. Such a theory of control by means of a gaze that objectifies, even when it is pulverized into micro-devices, is passé. With the simulation device we are no doubt as far from the strategy of transparence as the latter is from the immediate, symbolic operation of punishment which Foucault himself describes. Once again a spiral is missing here, the spiral in front of which Foucault, oddly enough, comes to a halt right at the threshold of a current revolution of the system which he has never wanted to cross.

One could say a lot about the central thesis of the book: there has never been a repression of sex but on the contrary an injunction against talking about it or voicing it and a compulsion to confess, to express, and to *produce* sex. Repression is only a trap and an alibi to hide assigning an entire culture to the sexual imperative. Supposing we agree with Foucault (note, however, that this assignation need in no way envy good old repression — and what difference does it make whether we say repression or an "induced" mode of speaking? It's only a question of terminology), what would remain of the book's essential idea? Basically this: it substitutes a negative, reactive, and transcendental conception of power which is founded on interdiction and law for a positive, active, and immanent conception, and this is in fact essential. One can only be struck by the coincidence between this new version of power and the new version of desire proposed by Deleuze and Lyotard: but there, instead of a lack or interdiction, one finds the deployment and the positive dissemination of flows and intensities. Such a coincidence is not accidental: *it's simply that in Foucault power takes the place of desire.* It is there in the same way as desire in Deleuze and Lyotard: always already there, purged of all negativity, a network, a rhizome, a contiguity diffracted ad infinitum. That is why there is no desire in Foucault: its place is already taken (looking at it the other way round, one way wonder if, in the schizoid and libidinal theories, desire or anything along that line is not the anamorphosis of a certain kind of power remaining under the sign of the same immanence, the same positivity, and the same machinery going every which way. Better yet, one can even wonder if, from one theory to the other, desire and power don't exchange their figure in ceaseless speculation — in mirror games that are for us games of truth).

These are certainly twin theories to their core; they are synchronous and isochronous in their "device" (*dispositif*: a term dear to them), and their facilitation (*frayage: Bahnung*) is the same — this is why they can be interchanged so well (see Deleuze's article on Foucault in *Critique*[3]) and can generate as of today all the by-products ("enjoyment of power," "the desire for capital," etc.) which are exact replicas of the previous generation's by-products ("the desire of revolution," "enjoyment of non-power," etc.). For in those days Reichians and Freudo-Marxists and desire and power were under opposite signs; today micro-desire (that of power) and micro-politics (that of desire) literally merge at the libido's mechanical confines: all one has to do is miniaturize. Such is the spiral Foucault suggests: power/knowledge/pleasure (he dare not say *desire*, although it is desire, the whole theory of desire, which comes directly into question). Foucault is part of this molecular intertwining which sketches out all of the future's visible hysteria: he has helped establish a systematic notion of power along the same operational lines as desire, just as Deleuze established a notion of desire along the lines of future forms of power. This collusion is too beautiful not to arouse suspicion, but it has in its behalf the quaint innocence of a betrothal. When power blends into desire and desire blends into power, let's forget them both.[4]

As for the hypothesis concerning repression, it's fine to object to it radically, but not on the basis of a simplistic definition. Yet what Foucault rejects is just such a repression of sex intended to channel all forms of energy toward material production. On this basis, it is too easy to say that the proletariat should have been the first class affected by repression, while history shows that the privileged classes first experienced it. In conclusion, the hypothesis concerning repression doesn't hold up. But it is the other hypothesis which is interesting: the hypothesis concerning a repression that originates from much farther away than the horizon of manufacturing and that simultaneously includes the whole horizon of sexuality. Whether we discuss the liberation of productive forces, of energies, or of speaking about sex, it is the same struggle and the same advancement toward an ever more powerful and differentiated socialization. One might as well say that repression in the maximal hypothesis, is never repression OF sex for the benefits of who knows what, but repression THROUGH sex (a grid of discourses, bodies, energies, and institutions imposed through sex, in the name of "the talking sex"). And sex which has been repressed only hides that repression by means of sex.

The production channel leads from work to sex, but only by switching tracks; as we move from political to "libidinal" economy (the last acquisition of '68), we change from a violent and archaic model of socialization (work) to a more subtle and fluid model which is at once more "psychic" and more in touch with the body (the sexual and the libidinal). There is a metamorphosis and a veering away from labor power to drive (*pulsion*), a veering away from a model founded on a system of representations (the famous "ideology") to a model operating on a system of affect (sex being only a kind of anamorphosis of the categorical social impera-tive). From one discourse to the other — since it really is a question of discourse — there runs the same ultimatum of *pro-duction* in the literal sense of the word. The original sense of "production" is not in fact that of material manufacture; rather, it means to render visible, to cause to appear and be made to appear: *pro-ducere*. Sex is produced as one produces a document, or as an actor is said to appear (*se produire*) on stage. To produce is to force what belongs to another order (that of secrecy and seduction) to mate-rialize. *Seduction* is that which is everywhere and always opposed to *production*; seduction with-draws something from the visible order and so runs counter to production, whose project is to set everything up in clear view, whether it be an object, a number, or a concept. Let everything be produced, be read, become real, visible, and marked with the sign of effectiveness; let every-thing be transcribed into force relations, into conceptual systems or into calculable energy; let everything be said, gathered, indexed and regis-tered: this is how sex appears in pornography, but this is more generally the project of our whole culture, whose natural condition is "obscenity." Ours is a culture of "monstration" and demonstration, of "productive" monstruosity (the "confession" so well analyzed by Foucault is one of its forms). We never find any seduction there — nor in pornography with its immediate production of sexual acts in a frenzied activation of pleasure; we find no seduction in those bodies penetrated by a gaze literally absorbed by the suction of the transparent void. Not a shadow of seduction can be detected in the universe of production, ruled by the transparency principle governing all forces in the order of visible and calculable phenomena: objects, machines, sexual acts, or gross national product.[5]

Pornography is only the paradoxal limit of the sexual, a realistic exacerbation and a mad obsession with the real — this is the "obscene," etymologically speaking and in all senses. But isn't the sexual itself a forced materialization, and isn't the coming of sexuality already part of the Western notion of what is real — the obsession peculiar to our culture with "instancing" and instrumentalizing all things? Just as it is absurd to separate in other cultures the religious, the economic, the political, the juridical, and even the social and other phantasmagorical categories, for the reason that they do not occur there, and because these concepts are like so many venereal diseases with which we infect them in order to "understand" them better, so it is also absurd to give autonomy to the sexual as "instance," and as an irreducible given to which all other "givens" can be reduced. We need to do a critique of sexual Reason, or rather a genealogy of sexual Reason, as Nietzsche has done a genealogy of Morals — because this is our new moral system. One could say of sexuality as of death: "It is a habit to which consciousness has not long been accustomed."

We do not understand, or we vaguely sympathize with, those cultures for which the sexual act has no finality in itself and for which sexuality does not have the deadly seriousness of an energy to be freed, a forced ejaculation, a production at all cost, or of a hygienic reckoning of the body. These are cultures which maintain long processes of seduction and sensuousness in which sexuality is one service among others, a long procedure of gifts and countergifts; lovemaking is only the eventual outcome of this reciprocity measured to the rhythm of an ineluctable ritual. For us, this no longer has any meaning: for us, *the sexual has become strictly the actualization of a desire in a moment of pleasure* —

all the rest is "literature." What an extraordinary crystallization of the orgastic function, which is itself the materialization of an energetic substance.

Ours is a culture of premature ejaculation. More and more, all seduction, all manner of seduction (which is itself a highly *ritualized* process), disappears behind the *naturalized* sexual imperative calling for the immediate realization of a desire. Our center of gravity has in fact shifted toward an unconscious and libidinal economy which only leaves room for the total naturalization of a desire bound either to fateful drives or to pure and simple mechanical operation, but above all to the imaginary order of repression and liberation.

Nowadays, one no longer says: "You've got a soul and you must save it," but: "You've got a sexual nature, and you must find out how to use it well."

"You've got an unconscious, and you must learn how to liberate it."

"You've got a body, and you must know how to enjoy it."

"You've got a libido, and you must know how to spend it," etc., etc.

This compulsion toward liquidity, flow, and an accelerated circulation of what is psychic, sexual, or pertaining to the body is the exact replica of the force which rules market value: capital must circulate; gravity and any fixed point must disappear; the chain of investments and reinvestments must never stop; value must radiate endlessly and in every direction. This is the form itself which the current realization of value takes. It is the form of capital, and sexuality as a catchword and a *model* is the way it appears at the level of bodies.

Besides, the body to which we constantly refer has no other reality than that of the sexual and productive model. It is capital which gives birth in the same movement to the energetic of labor power and to the body we dream of today as the locus of desire and the unconscious. This is the body which serves as a sanctuary for psychic energy and drives and which, dominated by these drives and haunted by primary processes, has itself become primary process — and thus an anti-body, the ultimate revolutionary referent. Both are simultaneously conceived in repression, and their apparent antagonism is yet another effect of repression. Thus, to rediscover in the secret of bodies an unbound "libidinal" energy which would be opposed to the bound energy of productive bodies, and to rediscover a phantasmal and instinctual truth of the body in desire, is still only to unearth the psychic metaphor of capital.

This is the nature of desire and of the unconscious: the trash heap of political economy and the psychic metaphor of capital. And sexual jurisdiction is the ideal means, in a fantastic extension of the jurisdiction governing private property, for assigning to each individual the management of a certain capital: psychic capital, libidinal capital, sexual capital, unconscious capital. And each individual will be accountable to himself for his capital, under the sign of his own liberation.

This is what Foucault tells us (in spite of himself): nothing functions with repression (*répression*), everything functions with production; nothing functions with repression (*refoulement*), everything functions with liberation. But *it is the same thing.* Any form of liberation is fomented by repression: the liberation of productive forces is like that of desire; the liberation of bodies is like that of women's liberation, etc. There is no exception to the logic of liberation: any force or any liberated form of speech constitutes one more turn in the spiral of power. This is how "sexual liberation" accomplishes a miracle by uniting in the same revolutionary ideal the two major effects of repression, liberation and sexuality.

Historically, this process has been building up for at least two centuries, but today it is in full bloom with the blessing of psychoanalysis — just as political economy and production have only made great strides with Marx's sanction and blessing. It is this conjecture which dominates us completely today, even through the "radical" contestation of Marx and psychoanalysis.*

---

*Because it is a partial critique, the *political* critique of Marx against the bureaucratic perversion of the revolution by revolutionary parties and against the economistic infrastructural perversion of the class struggle, etc., amounts to generalizing the axiomatic of production (productivity regarded as a discourse of total reference). This is Marxism's assumption in its purest form.

Likewise, because it is only partial, the *oedipal* critique of psychoanalysis (Deleuze, etc.) against the perversion of desire by the signifier, the law, castration, and the oedipal model only glorifies the axiomatic of desire and of the unconscious in its purest form.

It is in this way that the purified axioms of Marxism and psychoanalysis converge in today's only "revolutionary" catchword — that of the "productivity" of "desire." The "desiring machine" only fulfills, in one single movement, the positive destiny of Marxism and psychoanalysis. They at last come together under less naive

The category of the sexual and sexual discourse were born in the same way that the category of the clinical and the clinical gaze came into being —*there where there was nothing before* except uncontrolled, senseless, unstable, or highly ritualized forms. And where there was therefore *no repression either*, that leitmotiv by which we evaluate all earlier societies much more so than ours; we condemn them for being primitive from the technological point of view; these were repressed, non-"liberated" societies which did not even know of the unconscious. Psychoanalysis came to clear the way for sex by telling what was hidden — how incredible is the racism of truth, the evangeli-

---

auspices than Reich's, still too strongly marked by the Oedipus complex, the proletariat, repression, and class struggle. Reich had aimed too soon at the synthesis of two disciplines that were both historical and psychological and that were still cluttered with cumbersome elements: his mixture is archaic and his interpretation does not hold up; the times were not yet ready. But today, on the basis of a productivity cleansed of its contradictions, its historical objectives and its *determinations* and of a libido cleansed in its own way (of the Oedipus complex, repression, and of its too-genital, too-familial, *determinations*) the collusion and synthesis may finally be accomplished to each other's benefit: the mirror of production and that of desire will be able to refract each other endlessly.

cal racism of psychoanalysis; everything changes with the coming of the Word. If the question remains unsettled for our culture (repression or not), it is nonetheless without ambiguity for the others: they know neither repression nor the unconscious because they do not know the category of the sexual. We act as if the sexual were "repressed" wherever it does not appear in its own right: this is our way of saving sex through the "sex principle." It is our moral system (psychic and psychoanalytic) which remains hidden behind the hypothesis of repression and which governs our blindness. To talk about sexuality, "repressed" or not, "sublimated" or not, in feudal, rural, and primitive societies is a sign of utter foolishness (like reinterpreting religion, *ne varietur*, as ideology and mystification). And on that basis, then, it becomes possible again to say with Foucault: *there is not and there has never been any repression in our culture either* — not, however, according to his meaning, but in the sense that there has never truly been any sexuality. Sexuality, like political economy, is only *montage* (all of whose twists and turns Foucault analyzes); sexuality as we hear about it and as it "is spoken," even as the "id speaks," is only a simulacrum which experience has forever crossed up, baffled, and surpassed, as in any system. The coherence and transparence of *homo sexualis* has never had more reality than that of *homo oeconomicus.*

A long process simultaneously establishes the psychic, the sexual, and also the "other scene" of fantasy and the unconscious, as well as the energy to be produced there. Such psychic energy is but a direct effect of the "scenic" hallucination of repression through which energy is hallucinated as sexual substance; it will then become metaphorized and metonymized according to the various topical, economical, etc., instances and according to modalities of secondary, tertiary, etc., repression: what a marvellous edifice on the part of psychoanalysis, the loveliest hallucination of the world unseen, as Nietzsche would say. What an extraordinary effectiveness this model of energetic and scenic simulation possesses; what an extraordinary theoretical psychodrama is presented in this *mise-en-scène* of the psyche, this scenario of sex as an instance, as an eternal reality (as elsewhere others have hypostatized production into a generic dimension or driving energy). What does it matter whether the economic, the biological, or the psychic bears the cost of this *mise-en-scène* — or whether we refer to the "scene" or to the "other scene" — it is the scenario that counts, it is psychoanalysis in its entirety as a model of simulation which must be questioned.

In this production at all costs that is the modern sacrament of sex, there is such terrorism in the project of liquidation that one does not see why, unless it's for the beauty of the paradox, anyone would refuse to see repression there. Or could it be because this is too weak? Foucault doesn't want to talk about repression: but what else is that slow, brutal infection of the mind through sex, whose only equivalent in the past was infection through the soul (see Nietzsche — the infection through sex is nothing anyway but the historical and mental reversal of the infection through the soul under the sign of materialist parousia!)

But it is really useless to argue about the terms. One can say either way: speaking is the primary injunction and repression only a detour (in this sense, labor and exploitation are also only a detour and the alibi for something else more fundamental: no argument here), or repression comes first and speech is only a more modern variant of it ("repressive desublimation"). Basically, both hypotheses don't change much of

anything. What is disturbing in the first hypothesis (Foucault's) is that if there has been repression
somewhere, or at least the effect of repression (and
this can hardly be denied), then there is no way to
explain it. Why is the imaginary of repression
necessary for the balance of powers, if these live on
the induction, production, and extortion of speech?
On the other hand, one sees better why speech (a
metastable system) would come after repression,
which is only an unstable power system.

If sex exists solely when it is spoken and
discoursed about and when it is confessed, what was
there before we spoke about it? What break
establishes this discourse on sex, and in relationship
to what? We see what new powers are organized
around it, but what peripeteia of power instigates it?
What does it neutralize, or settle, or put to an end*

*According to Foucault, this break puts an end to "the
body and its pleasure," the innocence of libertinage, and
the *ars erotica* (of which we still retain a few terms, such as
seduction, charm, sensuality, enjoyment [*jouissance*],
"pleasure" itself — we no longer dare talk about
voluptuousness — terms which sex and psychoanalysis
have succeeded neither in annexing nor in discrediting
with their discourse). I think it puts an end to something
more radical, a configuration where not only sex and
desire but even the body and pleasure are not specified as
such, just as the discourse of production puts an end to a

(otherwise who can ever pretend to end it, as Foucault states on p. 157, "to break away from the agency of sex"[6])? Wherever we turn, it is not an innocent undertaking to "give meaning to sex"; power starts off from something (otherwise there would not even be those resistances noted on p. 96), something like an exclusion, a division, or a denial, and on that basis power can "produce something real" or produce *the* real. It is only from this point on that we can conceive of a new peripeteia of power — a catastrophic one this time — where power no longer succeeds in producing the real, in reproducing itself as real, or in opening new spaces to the reality principle, and where it falls into the hyperreal and vanishes: *this is the end of power*, the end of the strategy of the real.

For Foucault, the crisis or peripeteia of power does not even exist; there is only modulation, capillarity, a "micro-physical" segmentation of power as Deleuze says. And this is true: for Foucault, power operates right away like Monod's

regime where not only exchange value but also use value do not exist. Use value is the ultimate alibi, in sex as well as in production. And I'm afraid that in Foucault "pleasures" are still opposed to the "exchange value of the sexual" only insofar as they constitute the use value of the body.

genetic code, according to a diagram of dispersion and command (DNA), and according to a *teleonomical* order. Down with theological power, long live teleonomical power! Teleonomy is the end of all final determination and of all dialectic: it is the kind of generative inscription of the code that one expects — an immanent, ineluctable, and always positive inscription that yields only to infinitesimal mutations. If we look closely, power according to Foucault strangely resembles "this conception of social space which is as new as the recent conception of physical and mathematical spaces," as Deleuze says now that he has suddenly been blinded by the benefits of science. It is precisely this collusion that we must denounce, or laugh about. Everyone today wallows in the molecular as they do in the revolutionary. However, until further notice — and this could be the only one — the *true* molecule is not that of the revolutionaries; it is Monod's molecule of the genetic code and the "complex spirals of DNA." We should not, however, rediscover as an apparatus (*dispositif*) of desire what the cyberneticists have described as a matrix of code and of control.[7]

We see what benefit there is over the old finalist, dialectical, or repressive theories in supposing a total positivity, a teleonomy and a microphysics of power, but we must also see what we are getting into: a strange complicity with cybernetics which challenge precisely the same earlier schemas (Foucault does not, for that matter, hide his affinity with Jacob, Monod, and recently Jacques Ruffié, *De la Biologie à la Culture* [Paris: Flammarion, 1976]). The same can be said of Deleuze's molecular topology of desire, whose flows and connections will soon converge — if they have not already done so — with genetic simulations, microcellular drifts, and the random facilitations (*frayages*) of code manipulators. In the *Kafka: Pour une Littérature Mineure* (Paris: Editions de Minuit, 1975) of Deleuze-Guattari, the transcendental Law such as it is found in *The Castle* is opposed to the immanence of desire in the adjacent offices. How can we fail to see that the Law of the Castle has its "rhizomes" in the corridors and the offices — the "bar" or the break constituted by the law has simply been geared down ad infinitum in cellular and molecular succession. Desire is therefore only the molecular version of the Law. And what a strange coincidence to find schemas of desire and schemas of control everywhere. It is a spiral of power, of desire, and of the molecule which is now bringing us openly toward the final peripeteia of absolute control. Beware of the molecular!

This "veering away" in Foucault's writing occurs progressively since *Discipline and Punish*, going against *Madness and Civilization* and the whole original ordering of his genealogy. Why wouldn't sex, like madness, have gone through a confinement phase in which the terms of certain forms of reason and a dominant moral system were fomented before sex and madness, according to the logic of exclusion, once more became discourses of reference? Sex once more becomes the catchword of a new moral system; madness becomes the paradoxal form of reason for a society too long haunted by its absence and dedicated this time to its (normalized) cult under the sign of its own liberation. Such is also the trajectory of sex in the curved space of discrimination and repression where a *mise-en-scène* is installed as a long-term strategy to produce sex later as a new rule of the game. Repression or the *secret* is the locus of an imaginary inscription on whose basis madness or sex will subsequently become exchangeable as value.* Everywhere, as Foucault

---

*Sexual discourse is invented through repression, for repression speaks about sex better than any other form of discourse. Through repression (and only through repression), sex takes on reality and intensity because only

himself has so well demonstated, discrimination is the violent founding act of Reason — why wouldn't the same hold true of sexual reason?

This time we are in a full universe, a space radiating with power but also cracked, like a shattered windshield still holding together. However, this "power" remains a mystery — starting from despotic centrality, it becomes by the half-way point a "multiplicity of force relations" (but what is a force relation without a force resultant? It's a bit like Pere Ubu's polyhedra that set off in all directions like crabs) and it culminates, at the extreme pole, with *resistances* (what a divine surprise on pp. 95-96!) so small and so tenuous that, literally speaking, atoms of power and atoms of resistance merge at this microscopic level. The same fragment of gesture, body, gaze, and discourse encloses both the positive electricity of power and the negative electricity of resistance (and we wonder what the origin of that resistance might turn out to be; nothing in the book prepares us for it except the allusion to some inextricable "force relations." But since we may ask ourselves exactly the same question concerning power, a

---

confinement gives it the stature of myth. Its liberation is the beginning of its end.

balance is achieved in a discourse which in essence staunchly describes the only true spiral, that of its own power).

This is not an objection. It is a good thing that terms lose their meaning at the limits of the text (they don't do it enough).* Foucault makes the term *sex* and its true principle ("the fictive point of sex") lose their meaning; the analytics of power is not pushed to its conclusion at the point where power cancels itself out or where it has never been.

As economic reference loses its strength, either the reference of desire or that of power becomes preponderant. The reference of desire, born in psychoanalysis, comes to maturity in Deleuzian antipsychoanalysis under the form of a shattered molecular desire. The reference of power, which has a long history, is discussed again today by Foucault at the level of dispersed, interstitial power as a grid of bodies and of the ramiform pattern of controls. Foucault at least

---

*This is what a theory should be at best, rather than a statement of some truth, or above all a "breaking away from the agency of sex" — this is wishful thinking; and besides, if there is no repression, what does this emancipation mean? But we can bet that a new militant generation will rise over this horizon, brandishing "new procedures of truth."

economizes desire, as well as history (but being very prudent, he does not deny them), yet everything still comes back to *some kind of* power — without having that notion reduced and expurgated — just as with Deleuze everything comes back to *some kind of* desire, or with Lyotard to *some kind of* intensity: these are shattered notions, yet they remain miraculously intact in their current acceptance. Desire and intensity remain *force*/notions; with Foucault power remains, despite being pulverized, a *structural* and a polar notion with a perfect genealogy and an inexplicable presence, a notion which cannot be surpassed in spite of a sort of latent denunciation, a notion which is whole in each of its points or microscopic dots. It is hard to see how it could be reversed (we find the same aporia in Deleuze, where desire's reversion into its own repression is inexplicable). Power no longer has a *coup de force* — there is simply nothing else either on this side of it or beyond it (the passage from the "molar" or the "molecular" is for Deleuze still a *revolution* of desire, but for Foucault it is an anamorphosis of power). Only now Foucault does not see that power is dying (even infinitesimal power), that it is not just pulverized by pulverulent, that it is undermined by a reversal and tormented by a reversibility and a death which cannot appear in the genealogical process alone.

With Foucault, we always brush against political determination in its last instance. One form dominates and is diffracted into the models characteristic of the prison, the military, the asylum, and disciplinary action. This form is no longer rooted in ordinary relations of production (these, on the contrary are modeled after it); this form seems to find its procedural system within itself — and this represents enormous progress over the illusion of *establishing* power in a substance of production or of desire. Foucault unmasks all the final or causal illusions concerning power, but he does not tell us anything *concerning the simulacrum of power itself.* Power is an irreversible principle of organization because it fabricates the real (always more and more of the real), effecting a quadrature, nomenclature, and dictature without appeal; nowhere does it cancel itself out, become entangled in itself, or mingle with death. In this sense, even if it has no finality and no last judgment, power returns to its own identity again as a *final principle:* it is the last term, the irreducible web, the last tale that can be told; it is what structures the indeterminate equation of the word.

According to Foucault, this is the *come-on that power offers*, and it is not simply a discursive trap. What Foucault does not see is that power is never there and that its institution, like the institution of spatial perspective versus "real" space in the Renaissance, is only a simulation of perspective — it is no more reality than economic accumulation — and what a tremendous trap that is. Whether of time, value, the subject, etc., the axiom and the myth of a real or possible accumulation govern us everywhere, although we *know* that nothing is ever amassed and that stockpiles are self-consuming, like modern megapoleis, or like overloaded memories. Any attempt at accumulation is ruined in advance by the void.* Something in us disaccumulates unto death, undoes, destroys, liquidates, and disconnects so that we can resist the pressure of the real, and live. Something at the bottom of the whole system of production *resists the infinite expansion of production* — otherwise, we would all be already buried. There is something in power that resists as well, and we see no difference here between those who enforce it and those who

*It is this impossible accumulation which entails the equal impossibility of repression, for repression is only the inverse figure of accumulation — from the other side of the "bar."

submit to it: this distinction has become meaningless, not because the roles are interchangeable but because power is *in its form reversible*, because on one side and the other something holds out against the unilateral exercise and the infinite expansion of power, just as elsewhere against the infinite expansion of production. This resistance is not a "desire"; it is what causes power to come undone in exact proportion to its logical and irreversible extension. And it's taking place everywhere today.

In fact, the whole analysis of power needs to be reconsidered. To have power or not, to take it or lose it, to incarnate it or to challenge it: if this were power, it would not even exist. Foucault tells us something else; power is something that functions: ". . . power is not an institution, and not a structure; neither is it a certain strength we are endowed with; it is the name that one attributes to a complex strategical situation in a particular society" (*The History of Sexuality*, p. 93). Neither central, nor unilateral, nor dominant, power is distributional; like a vector, it operates through relays and transmissions. Because it is an immanent, unlimited field of forces, we still do not understand what power runs into and against what it stumbles since it is expansion, pure magnetization. However, if power were this magnetic

infiltration ad infinitum of the social field, it
would long ago have ceased meeting with any
resistance. Inversely, if it were the one-sidedness
of an act of submission, as in the traditional
"optic," it would long ago have been overthrown
everywhere. It would have collapsed under the
pressure of antagosnistic forces.

Yet this has never happened, apart from a few
"historical" exceptions. For "materialist" thinking, this can only appear to be an internally
insoluble problem: why don't "dominated" masses
immediately overthrow power? Why fascism?
Against this unilateral theory (but we understand why it survives, particularly among "revolutionaries" — they would really like power
for themselves), against this native vision, but
also against Foucault's functional vision in
terms of relays and transmissions, we must say
that *power is something that is exchanged*. Not in
the economical sense, but in the sense that
power is executed according to a reversible cycle
of seduction, challenge, and ruse (neither axis
nor indefinite relay, but a cycle). And if power
cannot be exchanged in this sense, it purely and
simply disappears. We must say that power
seduces, but not in the vulgar sense of a complicit
form of desire on the part of those who are

dominated — this comes down to basing it in the *desire of others*, which is really going overboard in taking people for idiots — no, power seduces by that reversibility which haunts it, and upon which a minimal symbolic cycle is set up. Dominators and dominated exist no more than victims and executioners. (While exploiters and exploited do in fact exist, they are on different sides because there is no reversibility in production, which is precisely the point: nothing essential happens at that level.) With power there are no antagonistic positions: it is carried out according to a cycle of seduction.

The one-sidedness of a force relation never exists, a one-sidedness upon which a power "structure" might be established, or a form of "reality" for power and its perpetual movement, which is linear and final in the traditional vision but radiating and spiraling in Foucault. Unilateral or segmentary: this is the dream of power imposed on us by reason. But nothing yearns to be that way; everything seeks its own death, including power. Or rather — but this is the same thing — everything wants to be exchanged, reversed, or abolished in a cycle (this is in fact why neither repression nor the unconscious exists: reversibility is always already there). *That alone is what seduces deep down*, and that alone constitutes pure gratification (*jouissance*), while power only satisfies a particular form of hegemonic logic belonging to reason. Seduction is elsewhere.

Seduction is stronger than power because it is a reversible and mortal process, while power wants to be irreversible like value, as well as cumulative and immortal like value. Power shares all the illusions of the real and of production; it wants to belong to the order of the real and so falls over into the imaginary and into self-superstition (helped by theories which analyze it even if only to challenge it). Seduction, however, does not partake of the real order. It never belongs to the order of force or to force relations. It is precisely for this reason that seduction envelops the whole *real* process of power, as well as the whole *real* order of production, with this never-ending reversibility and disaccumulation — without which *neither power nor production would even exist.*

Behind power, or at the very heart of power and of production, there is a void which gives them today a last glimmer of reality. Without that which reverses them, cancels them, and seduces them, they would never have attained reality.

Besides, the real has never interested anyone. It is the locus of disenchantment par
excellence, the locus of simulacrum of accumulation against death. Nothing could be worse. It
is the imaginary catastrophe standing behind
them that sometimes makes reality and the truth
fascinating. Do you think that power, economy,
sex — all the *real's* big numbers — would have
stood up one single instant without a fascination
to support them which originates precisely in
the inversed mirror where they are reflected and
continually reversed, and where their imaginary
catastrophe generates a tangible and immanent
gratification? `

Today especially, the real is no more than a
stockpile of dead matter, dead bodies, and dead
language. It still makes us feel,secure today to
evaluate this *stock of what is real* (let's not talk
about energy: the ecological complaint hides the
fact that it is not material energy which is
disappearing on the species' horizon but the
energy of the real, the reality of the real and of
every serious possibility, capitalistic or revolutionary, of managing the real). If the horizon of
production has vanished, then the horizon of
speech, sexuality, or desire can still carry on;

there will always be something to liberate, to enjoy, and to exchange with others through words: now that's real, that's substantial, that's prospective stock. That's power.

Not so, unfortunately. Not for long, that is. This sort of thing consumes itself as it goes along. We have made, and have wanted to make, an irreversible agency (*instance*) out of both sex and power; and out of desire we have made a force or irreversible energy (a *stock* of energy, needless to say, since desire is never far from capital). For we give meaning, following our use of the imaginary, only to what is irreversible; accumulation, progress, growth, production, value, power, and desire itself are all irreversible processes — inject the slightest dose of reversibility into our economical, political, institutional, or sexual machinery (*dispositif*) and everything collapses at once. This is what endows sexuality today with this mythic authority over bodies and hearts. But it is also what makes it fragile, like the whole structure of production.

Seduction is stronger than production. It is stronger than sexuality and must never be confused with it. It is not an internal process of sexuality, although it is generally reduced to that. It is a circular and reversible process of challenge, one-upmanship, and death. The sexual, on the contrary, is the form of seduction that has been reduced and restricted to the energetic terms of desire.

What we need to analyze is the intrication of the process of seduction with the process of production and power and the irruption of a minimum of reversibility in every irreversible process, secretly ruining and dismantling it while simultaneously insuring that minimal continuum of pleasure moving across it and without which it would be nothing. And we must keep in mind that production everywhere and always seeks to exterminate seduction in order to establish itself over the single economy governing force relations; we must also keep in mind that sex or its production seeks everywhere to exterminate seduction in order to establish itself over the single economy governing relations of desire.

When Jesus arose from the dead, he became a Zombi.

Graffito, Watts, Los Angeles

The Messiah will only come when he will no longer be necessary. He will come one day after his advent. He will not come on the day of the Last Judgment, but on the day after.

Kafka

Thus will they await the Messiah, not only on the day after, but on all the following days, even though he was already there. Or in other words: God was already dead long before they knew it, just as light-years separate the same event from one star to the next, thereby separating advent from event.

Thus will they always be one Revolution late. Or rather: they will await the Revolution to the very day, even though it has already been accomplished. And when it happens, it will be because it is no longer necessary; it will be nothing more than the sign of what has already occurred.

Are the Messiah and the Revolution so

insignificant that they must always arrive late, like a projected shadow or a reality effect after the fact, whereas things have never needed the Messiah or a Revolution in order to take place?

But in the end the Revolution signifies only this: that it has already taken place and that it had a meaning just before, one day before, but not anymore now. When it comes, it is to hide the fact that it is no longer meaningful.

In fact, the revolution has already taken place. Neither the bourgeois revolution nor the communist revolution: just the revolution. This means that an entire cycle is ending, and they have not noticed it. And they will play the game of linear revolution, whereas it has already curved upon itself to produce its simulacrum, like stucco angels whose extremities join in a curved mirror.

All things come to an end in their re-doubled simulation — a sign that a cycle is completed. When the reality effect, like the useless day-after Messiah, starts uselessly duplicating the course of things, it is the sign that a cycle is ending in an interplay of simulacra where everything is replayed before death, at which point everything falls over far behind the horizon of truth.

It is useless therefore to run after power or to discourse about it *ad infinitum* since from now on it also partakes of the sacred horizon of appearances and is also there only to hide the fact that it no longers exists, or rather to indicate that since the apogee of the political has been crossed, the other side of the cycle is now starting in which power reverts into its own simulacrum.

Power is no more held than a secret is extracted, for the secrecy of power is the same as that of the secret: it does not exist. On the other side of the cycle — the side of the decline of the real — only the *mise-en-scène* of the secret, or of power, is operational. But this is the sign that the substance of power, after a ceaseless expansion of several centuries, is brutally exploding and that the sphere of power is in the process of contracting from a star of first magnitude to a red dwarf, and then to a black hole absorbing all the substance of the real and all the surrounding energies, now transmuted at once into a single pure sign — the sign of the social whose density crushes us.

Neither an agency (*instance*), a structure, a substance, nor in fact a force relation, power is a challenge. From the power puppet of primitive societies which talks but has nothing to say to the current form of power which is there only to exorcise the absence of power, a whole cycle has been covered which is one of a double challenge, the challenge of power against all of society and the challenge against those who hold power. This is the secret history both of power and its catastrophe.

Let us consider the *real* history of capital. All materialist critical thought is only the attempt to *stop* capital, to freeze it in the moment of its economic and political rationality. Capital's "mirror phase," lulled by the sirens of dialectics. Of course at this point materialist thinking also freezes everything that resists it at this one phase. Fortunately, capital does not remain trapped in this model but goes beyond it in its irrational movement to leave standing there an example of materialist thought curled back upon its nostalgic dialectics and its already lost idea of the revolution. Such thought was in essence only a rather superficial moment of theory, but above all it operated like a brake in attempting to neutralize, with a well-tempered *socialité* and an ideal social transparence, the deep-rooted opposition and *deadly challenge to the social itself.*

Today the extremes finally come face to face,

once the conservative obstacle of critical thought has been removed. Not only do social *forces* clash (however dominated by one single great model of socialization), but *forms* come into opposition as well — the forms of capital and of sacrifice, of value and of challenge — *with the death of the social at stake.* The social itself must be considered a model of simulation and a form to be overthrown since it is a strategic form of value brutally positioned by capital and then idealized by critical thought. And we still do not know what it is that forever has fought against it and that irresistibly destroys it today.

All forms of power have endeavored to camouflage this fundamental challenge in the form of force relations such as dominator/dominated and exploiter/exploited, thereby channeling all resistance into a frontal relation (even reduced to microstrategies, this conception still dominates in Foucault: the puzzle of guerilla warfare has simply been substituted for the chessboard of classical battle). For in terms of force relations, power always wins, even if it changes hands as revolutions come and go.

But it is doubtful if anyone has ever thought it possible to exorcise power by force. Rather, each person knows deep down that any form of power is a personal challenge, a challenge to the death, and one that can only be answered by a counterchallenge to break the logic of power or, even better, to enclose it in a circular logic. Such is the nature of this counterchallenge — nonpolitical, nondialectical, and nonstrategic — but whose strength throughout history has nonetheless been incalculable: this is the challenge which dares those who hold power to exercise it to the limit and which can only spell death for those who are dominated. A challenge to power to be power, power of the sort that is total, irreversible, without scruple, and with no limit to its violence. No form of power dares go that far (to the point where in any case it too would be destroyed). And so it is in facing this unanswerable challenge that power starts to break up.

There was a time when power allowed itself to be sacrificed according to the rules of this symbolic game from which it cannot escape. A time when power possessed the ephemeral and mortal quality of what had to be sacrificed. Ever since it has sought to escape that rule, or has ceased being a *symbolic* power in order to become a *political* power and a strategy of social domination, the symbolic challenge has not stopped haunting power in the political sense, nor has it stopped undoing the truth of the political. Now that it has been struck by that challenge, the entire substance of the political is crumbling. We are at the point where no one exercises power or wants it anymore, not because of some historical or temperamental weakness but because its secret has been lost, and no one wants to take up the challenge any longer. How true it is, then, that power need only be enclosed within power for it to burst.

Against that "strategy" which is not a strategy, power has defended itself in every possible way (this is exactly what constitutes its practice): by being democratized, liberalized, vulgarized, and, more recently, decentralized and deterritorialized, etc. But whereas force relations become easily trapped and deenergized by these tricks of the political, the reverse challenge, with its ineluctable simplicity, comes to an end only with power.

People always reason in terms of strategies and force relations; they don't see the desperate effort of the oppressed to escape oppression or uproot power. They never measure the extraordinary force of the challenge because this challenge is unremitting and invisible (although that force can manifest itself in large-scale acts, but acts "without objective, without duration, and without future"). The challenge is hopeless — but then hope is a weak value, and history itself is a value degraded through time and distorted between its end and its means. All the stakes of history are eluctable, negotiable, and *dialectic*. Challenge is the opposite of *dialogue*: it creates a nondialectic, ineluctable space. It is neither a means nor an end: it opposes its own space to political space. It knows neither middle-range nor long-term; its only term is the immediacy of a response or of death. Everything linear, including history, has an end; challenge alone is without end since it is indefinitely reversible. And it is this reversibility which gives it its prodigious force.*

*This is no doubt the same reversibility which the category of the feminine has exerted on the masculine throughout the entire course of our culture's sexual history: thus the challenge which the feminine offers the masculine of taking its pleasure (*jouissance*) alone, and of alone exercising the right to pleasure and sex. Women's right to reserve sex and to deny pleasure, their constant reversals, and their continuous refraction of sexual power into the void have always exerted an incalculable pressure, with no possibility of response from the "strong" masculine side except through a headlong flight into

No one has ever seriously considered this other, nonpolitical side of power, the side of its symbolic reversal. However, because it lacks definition by the void, this oppositional challenge has always been in play and has overcome in the end power's political definition as central, legislative, or police power. It is also in play at the current stage, where power only appears as a sort of curvature of social space, or the summation of scattered particles, or the branching out of random elements "in cluster" (any term from microphysics or computer theory can be transfered today into power, as well as into desire). This is a stage of power, *a la Foucault*, the conductor, inductor, and strategist of speech. But the turn-around Foucault manages from power's repressive centrality to its shifting positivity is only a peripeteia. We stay effectively within political discourse — "we never get out of it," says Foucault — although we need precisely to grasp the radical lack of definition in the notion of the political, its lack of existence, its simulation, and

---

phallocracy. Today phallocracy is crumbling under this very challenge, taking with it all forms of traditional sexuality — and not at all due to social pressure from any sort of feminine liberation.

what from that point on sends the mirror of the void back to power. In effect, we need a symbolic violence more powerful than any political violence.

Let us consider now the *real* history of class struggle whose only moments were those when the dominated class fought on the basis of its self-denial "as such," on the basis of the sole fact that it amounted to nothing. Marx had told it that it should be abolished one day, but this was still a political perspective. When the class itself, or a fraction of it, prefers to act as a radical non-class, or as the lack of existence of a class, i.e., to act out its own death right away within the explosive structure of capital, when it chooses to implode suddenly instead of seeking political expansion and class hegemony, then the result is June '48, the Commune, or May '68. The secret of the void lies here, in the incalculable force of the implosion (contrary to our imaginary concept of revolutionary explosion) — think of the Latin Quarter on the afternoon of May 3.

Power did not always consider itself as power, and the secret of the great politicians was to know that power *does not exist*. To know that it is only a perspectival space of simulation, as was the pictorial Renaissance, and that if power seduces, it is precisely — what the naive realists of politics will never understand — because it is simulacrum and because it undergoes a metamorphosis into signs and is invented on the basis of signs. (This is why *parody*, the reversal of signs or their hyperextension, can touch power more deeply than any force relation.) This secret of power's lack of existence that the great politicians shared also belongs to the great bankers, who know that money is nothing, that money does not exist; and it also belonged to the great theologians and inquisitors who knew that God does not exist, that God is dead. This gives them incredible superiority. Power is truly sovereign when it grasps this secret and confronts itself with that very challenge. When it ceases to do so and pretends to finds a truth, a substance, or a representation (in the will of the people, etc.), then it loses its sovereignty, allowing others to hurl back the challenge of its own life or death, until it dies in effect at the hands of that infatuation with itself, that imaginary concept of itself, and that superstitious belief in itself as a substance; it dies as well when it fails to recognize (*méconnaissance*) itself as a void, or as something reversible in death. At one time leaders were killed when they lost that secret.

When one talks so much about power, it's because it can no longer be found anywhere. The same goes for God: the stage in which he was everywhere came just before the one in which he was dead. Even the death of God no doubt came before the stage in which he was everywhere. The same goes for power, and if one speaks about it so much and so well, that's because it is deceased, a ghost, a puppet; such is also the meaning of Kafka's words: the Messiah of the day after is only a God resuscitated from among the dead, a zombi. The finesse and the microscopic nature of the analysis are themselves a "nostalgia effect." And so everywhere we see power coupled with seduction (it's almost obligatory these days) in order to give it a second existence. Power gets its fresh blood from desire. And it's no longer anything more than a sort of "desire effect" at the confines of the social, or a sort of "strategy effect" at the confines of history. It is here also that "the" powers of Foucault come into play: grafted upon the privacy of bodies, the tracing of discourses, the facilitation of gestures, in a more insinuating, more subtle, and more discursive strategy which there too takes away power from history and brings it nearer to seduction.

This universal fascination with power in its exercise and its theory is so intense because it is a fascination with a *dead* power characterized by a simultaneous "resurrection effect," in an obscene and parodic mode, of all the forms of power already seen — exactly like sex in pornography. The imminence of the death of all the great referents (religious, sexual, political, etc.) is expressed by exacerbating the forms of violence and representation that characterized them. There is no doubt that fascism, for example, is the first obscene and pornographic form of a desperate "revival" of political power. As the violent reactivation of a form of power that despairs of its rational foundations (the form of representation that was emptied of its meaning during the course of the nineteenth and twentieth centuries), as the violent reactivation of the social in a society that despairs of its own rational and contractual foundation, fascism is nevertheless the only fascinating modern form of power: it is the only one since Machiavelli to assert itself as such, as a challenge, by trifling with all forms of political "truth," and it is the only one to have taken up the challenge to assume power unto death (whether its own or that of others). Besides, it is because it has taken up the challenge that fascism has benefited from this strange consent, this absence of resistance to power. Why have all the *symbolic* resistances failed in the face of fascism — a unique fact in history? No ideological mystification and no sexual repression *à la Reich* can explain it. Only challenge can arouse such a passion for responding to it, such a frenzied assent to play the game in return, and thus raise every resistance. This, moreover, remains a mystery: why does one respond to a challenge? For what reason does one accept to play better, and feel passionately compelled to answer such an arbitrary injunction?

Fascist power is then the only form which was able to reenact the ritual prestige of death, but (and most importantly here) in an already posthumous and phony mode, a mode of one-upmanship and *mise-en-scène*, and in an *aesthetic* mode — as Benjamin clearly saw — that was no longer truly sacrificial. Fascism's politics is an aesthetics of death, one that already has the look of a nostalgia fad; and everything that has had this look since then must be inspired by fascism, understood as an *already nostalgic* obscenity and violence, as an already reactionary scenario of power and death which is already obsolete the very moment it appears in history. Again, an eternal shift in the advent of the Messiah, as Kafka says. An eternal inner simulation of power, which is never already (*jamais déjà*) anything but the sign of what it was.

We find the same nostalgia and the same simulation characteristic of nostalgia fads when we look today at "micro" fascisms and "micro" powers. The "micro" operator can only down-shift from what fascism may have been without resolving it and transform an extremely complex scenario of simulation and death into a simplified "floating signifier," "whose essential function is denunciation" (Foucault). Its function is also invocation because the memory of fascism (like the memory of power), even in the micro-form, is still the nostalgic invocation of the political, or *of a form of truth for the political*; and its invocation simultaneously allows us to save the hypothesis of desire, whose mere paranoic accident power and fascism can always appear to be.

In any case, power lures us on and truth lures us on. Everything is in the lightning-quick contraction in which an entire cycle of accumulation, of power, or of truth comes to a close. There is never any inversion or any subversion: the cycle must be accomplished. But it can happen instantaneously. It is death that is at stake in this contraction.

Notes

1. *Art Press* 22 (January-February, 1976): 3, [Translator's note]

2. Roland Barthes, *L'Empire des signes* (Geneva, 1970), p. 43, where Barthes writes, ". . . in Japan . . . sexuality is in sex and not elsewhere; in the United States, it is the opposite: sex is everywhere except in sexuality." [Translator's note]

3. Gilles Deleuze, "Ecrivain Non: Un Nouveau Cartographe," *Critique* 31 (1975): 1207-27. [Translator's note]

4. See Gilles Deleuze and Félix Guattari, *Anti-Oedipus: Capitalism and Schizophrenia*, trans. R. Hurley, M. Seem, and H. Lane (New York, 1977) and Jean-François Lyotard, *Economie Libidinale* (Paris, 1974). [Translator's note]

5. For a more complete account of Baudrillard's critique of production, see his *Mirror of Production*, trans. Mark Poster (St. Louis, 1975); for a fuller discussion of production/seduction, see his recent *De la séduction* (Paris, 1979), esp. pp. 57-73. [Translator's note]

6. *The History of Sexuality*, vol.1, *An Introduction*, trans. Robert Hurley (New York, 1978). [Translator's note]

7. See Jacques Monod, *Chance and Necessity: An Essay on the Natural Philosophy of Biology*, trans. Austryn Wainhouse (New York, 1971). [Translator's note]

Translated by Nicole Dufresne

Forget Baudrillard
An Interview with Sylvere Lotringer

"As in judo, the best answer to an adversary maneuver is not to retreat, but to go along with it, turning it to one's own advantage, as a resting point for the next phase."
Michel Foucault

—

Chapter One

The Ends of History—Hyperreality—Nihilism and Disenchantment— Neutralizing Desire—Appearance and Disappearance—Sexuality and Obscenity—Foucault: Genealogy and Simulation—Desire and Seduction—Metaphor and Metamorphosis—The Disappearance of the Subject—The Giddiness of Chance—Panic and Information

Sylvere Lotringer: Let's begin at the end or, rather, at the ends: the end of production, the end of history, the end of the political. Your reflections begin with a series of liquidations. Has the time come to put Western civilization in the wax museum? Is everything now for sale?

Jean Baudrillard: I don't know if it's a question of an "end". The word is probably meaningless in any case, because we're no longer so sure that there is such a thing as linearity. I would prefer to begin,

67

even if it sounds a little like science fiction, with a quotation from *Die Provinz des Menschen* (The Human Province), a recent book by Elias Canetti.[1] It is possible, he says—and he finds the idea rather painful—that starting from a precise moment in time the human race has dropped out of history. Without even being conscious of the change, we suddenly left reality behind. What we have to do now, continues Canetti, would be to find that critical point, that blind spot in time. Otherwise, we just continue on with our self-destructive ways. This hypothesis appeals to me because Canetti doesn't envisage an end, but rather what I would hall an "ecstasy", in the primal sense of that word—a passage at the same time into the dissolution and the transcendence of a form.

SL: *History survives its disappearance, but somewhere its spirit got snatched away ...*

JB: History isn't over, it is in a state of simulation, like a body that's kept in a state of hibernation. In this irreversible coma everything continues to function all the same, and eventually can even seem to amount to history. And then, surreptitiously (as Canetti has it), it's possible that everything is no longer real or true. In any case we would no longer be in a position to decide on that.

SL: *The "end" you're talking about would be the end of all finalities—together with an exacerbated, empty parody of their resurgence.*

JB: There is no end in the sense that God is dead, or history is dead. I would prefer not to play the role of the lugubrious, thoroughly useless prophet. It is not a tragic event, something highly charged with emotion, something that you could mourn—for there would still be something to be done about it. Suddenly, there is a curve in the road, a turning point. Somewhere, the real scene has been lost, the scene where you had rules for the game and some solid stakes that everybody could rely on.

SL: *How did that happen? Has this really happened?*

JB: That's fiction. History has stopped meaning, referring to anything—whether you call it social space or the real. We have passed into a kind of hyper-real where things are being replayed *ad infinitum.*

SL: *Traditional societies had no history but they had a mythology; we're discovering now that history may have been our own mythology. If we can cease believing in history, then maybe history had more to do with faith than fact.*

JB: But then, what does it mean "to believe?" That would mean maintaining some kind of subjectivity as a criterion of the validity of things. Now if credibility alone is what gives things meaning, then we're bound to remain trapped in the imaginary.

What interests me instead (but can you still call this history?) is the possibility of a pure event, an event that can no longer be manipulated, interpreted, or deciphered by any historical subjectivity.

SL: *Can individual subjectivity be totally short-circuited by the event?*

JB: The problematic of the subject implies that reality can still be represented, that things give off signs guaranteeing their existence and significance—in short, that there is a reality principle. All of that is now collapsing with the dissolution of the subject. This is the well-known "crisis of representation". But just because this system of values is coming apart—the system which also supported the political and theatrical scenes—that doesn't mean we are being left in a complete void. On the contrary, we are confronted with a more radical situation.

SL: The tabula rasa brings out tendencies latent in the culture. It clears the ground. But there is a high price to pay in terms of emptiness and disenchantment. There you have all the seduction, and the sadness, of nihilism.

JB: It is true that logic only leads to disenchantment. We can't avoid going a long way with negativity, with nihilism and all. But then don't you think a more exciting world opens up? Not a more reassuring world, but certainly more thrilling, a world where the name of the game remains secret. A world ruled by reversibility and indetermination ...

SL: That's certainly radical; it leaves no roots.

JB: Radicality is not a more sublime virtue of theory. It means isolating in things whatever allows for interpretation, whatever overburdens them with meaning. I don't derive any malicious pleasure from this analysis; still, it gives me a curious sense of giddiness ...

SL: But who's there to feel giddy? To exult in one's own disappearance is still another, more paradoxical, paroxystic form of subjectivity. What's left once you've liquidated that overload of meaning?

JB: What remains is a good deal less than one would like to admit. Every system of value—in terms of energy, for example—seems to be crumbling down.

SL: You settled your score with Marx in The Mirror of Production[2]. *Why haven't you written a* Mirror of Desire *to have done with the judgment of Freud?*

JB: I can't bring myself to write something on psychoanalysis. It would be useless to attack frontally its ideology or proclaim its demise. You have to allow desire to catch itself in its own trap.

SL: Desire was caught from the start. That's the reactive side of any theory. You can only reveal a phenomenon if it is already disappearing. Where is hysteria now? Nowhere and everywhere. Often the pyramid of concepts is piled up sky high on top of an empty tomb.

JB: It is always the same sign that controls appearance and disappearance. It presides over both. In the meantime, you're left to your own devices. There may be events, there may be a history...

SL: The history of sexuality, for example.

JB: Sexuality has gone weightless. It is now reaching the state of "obscenity." But everyone conspires to mask its disappearance by setting up *trompe l'oeil* stage decore.[3]

SL: Psychoanalysis pretends to cure sexual neurosis,

while it keeps on injecting it with a semblance of reality. Although far removed from the Freudian point of view, Foucault still participates in that nostalgic effect of theory. After all, paying so much attention to the genealogy of sexuality accredits the idea that it is still a space to be occupied. But it is more like Grand Central Station ...

JB: I don't see the point of retracing the genealogy of sexuality. It's so true, so undeniable that there is nothing to say about it.

SL: American sexuality is more Foucaldian than Foucault. In sex clinics here, masturbation has become a categorical imperative if you want to reach a synthetic genitality. Your position with respect to Foucault is of the same order. Foucault wrote the archeology of things; you take them to the point of their cryogenicization. In L'Ordre des Simulacres (The Order of Simulation), *though your approach was pretty close to his . . .*[4]

JB: You're talking about the three orders? I could have made a book out of it, others rushed in to find examples. As for myself, without denying it, I don't believe it holds up. For a time I believed in Foucaldian genealogy, but the order of simulation is antinomical to genealogy.

SL: An anti-genealogy then?

JB: No. If you take this logic to the extreme,

what you get is the reabsorption of all genealogy. That's why I believe Foucault was unable to make the leap. What interests me is the mysterious point where he stops and finds nothing more to say.

SL: You keep criss-crossing Gilles Deleuze and Felix Guattari's path, breaking away from representation, rejecting dialectics, dismissing meaning and metaphor. You part company with them on the terrain of subjectivity: they put the subject in flux, you abolish it. They make desire the basis of becoming; you see becoming as annihilating desire.

JB: I couldn't care less about desire. I neither want to abolish it nor to take it into consideration. I wouldn't know where to put it anymore.

SL: That's no surprise. You derive your own energy from the collapse of values. To make desire itself the basis of the system becomes redundant.

JB: What bothers me about desire is the idea of an energy at the source of all these fluxes. Is desire really involved? In my opinion, it has nothing to do with it.

SL: Well then, what does?

JB: Earlier on you mentioned disenchantment. The other, enchanting aspect, for me, is no longer desire, that is clear. It is seduction. Things make events all by themselves, without any mediation, by a sort of instant commutation. There is no longer any metaphor, rather metamorphosis. Metamorphosis abolishes metaphor, which is the mode of language, the possibility of communicating meaning. Metamorphosis is at the radical point of the system, the point where there is no longer any law or symbolic order. It is a process without any subject, without death, beyond any desire, in which only the rules of the game of forms are involved. Among other things, what psychoanalysis has to say about mythology is an abuse of metaphorical language.

SL: And what would correspond to that mythology in the order of metamorphosis?

JB: The possibility of transmutation: becoming-animal, becoming-woman. What Gilles Deleuze says about it seemed to me to fit perfectly.[5]

Love is no longer considered as a dependence of desire upon a lack, but in the unconscious form of the transformation into the other. In that metamorphic unconscious nothing is repressed. The metaphor is by-passed. Conversly, in metastasis — the proliferation of bodies, obesity, cancer—there again, unfortunately, the subject no longer exists. There is no more language. Metaphor is no longer possible.

SL: *And what do you see taking shape with the disappearance of subjectivity?*

JB: Something rather paradoxical. There are three modes of disappearance. Either the subject disappears in the cloning system, eliminating death. That has no charm. It is too much like an extermination which is the proliferating meta-static form of the disappearance of the other. Or, you could have disappearance as death, which is the metaphorical form of the subject. Or else, disapppearance as a game, the art of disappearance.

SL: *Alongside these modes of disappearance, the mechanical (cloning), organic (death), and ritual (game) forms, why not conceive of a more lively way of disappearing? The possibility of assuming roles without identifying with them. One agrees to disappear, but like nomads, in order to reappear somewhere else, where one is not expected.*

JB: I conceive of that disappearance abstractly, with Deleuze, as a flux, but also as an absolute transparency. It is the loss of the real, the absolute distance of the real. One can no longer touch things.

SL: *The only form of the real that remains, as I see it, is a shifting between things. Otherwise you are paralyzed—or vaporized. Paralysis is the panicky plea for identity. It's neurosis: wearing yourself out trying to pour into concrete what is slipping away in all directions. Evaporation is chloroform, or ether. Disappearing without a trace. It chills you to the bone; it puts you to sleep, too.*

JB: It's possible that in places like New York people can remain in a kind of positive, happy fluidity, a state of trans-pearing. But most people experience it as a kind of liquid terror.

SL: *Is it worth abdicating all subjectivity in order to protect ourselves from terror?*

JB: We're no longer in systems of real accomplishment; today they are necessarily potential, with the added bonus of risk, panic. **The de-subjectification of things.**

SL: *What's there to risk if all subjectivity is being extinguished?*

JB: We're condemned to effects of giddiness —in all the electronic games as well. There's no more pleasure, no more interest, but a kind of dizziness induced by the connections, the switching operations in which the subject gets lost. You manipulate all you want, without any objective, with the effect of aleatory giddiness of the potential systems where anything can happen.

SL: You prefer panic to terror.

JB: Panic doesn't have to be unhappy. I see it as ecstasy. It's just a mode of propagation by contiguity, like contagion, only faster—the ancient principle of metamorphosis, going from one form to another without passing through a system of meaning. This process of effects in the absence of causes is a form of extraordinary expansion. The "speed" that Virilio talks about. is an effect of panic with respect to movement.[6]

A giddiness effect. Panic can also be the inflation of the event by the news media. All the communication theories have to be revised, including my own, which is still too meaningful. People no longer seek to appropriate things, or even destroy them. Bataille's "devil's share" was still part of the ultimate romanticism of political economy. Now it's something else.[7]

Chapter Two

Death and Metastasis — The Giddiness of Theory — Desire and Culture — "Objective" Necessity — Sociology and Metaphysics — The End of the Social — The Symbolic Exchange and Destiny — The Fatal Between Chance and Necessity — Movement and Speed — The Ecstasy of Capital — Gambling as Extermination of Value — Statistics and Fate — Objective Chance without the Unconscious — The Chain of Appearances

SL: *What do you make of death? Of the three modes of disappearance, it's clearly the one you are least interested in. It doesn't disappear for all that...*

JB: Death has passed into either the history of metamorphoses or into metastatic history. I found an article by Franz Bader, a German writer from the early 19th century, entitled "On Ecstasy as Metastasis." For him ecstasy is the anticipation of death, a passage into the metastatic state of the living subject. Death is replaced by the passage of this point of inertia.

SL: *Every time I meet William Burroughs, I feel I'm in the presence of a happy dead man. As a living person he seems rather bored. I asked him if he would go to the moon. "Of course," he replied. "I'd go anywhere; I'd leave the solar system if they came to get me in a flying saucer." "Even if there is no coming back?" I asked. He looked at me. "Why come back?"*

JB: I experienced the same feeling of no return during a trip to the United States a few years ago. It was a real shock. I had the revelation that I was entering the period of the rest of my life from another point of view, in a state of complete irony with respect to what had gone before. When there is no fundamental passion, when life or love disappears, there is no longer any possibility of a multiplicity of modalities, with respect to love or existence. It's an extra helping, a little bit ecstatic, a little bit residual, but also profoundly melancholic. Death is an event that has always already taken place.

SL: *I've often wondered how one could live theories like yours.*

JB: I got into it fairly late. For a long time, I was very "cool" about producing theories. Of course there had to be an obsession behind it, but I didn't think it had very much to do with anything. It was a kind of game. I could write about death without it having any influence whatsoever on my life. When someone asked me, "What can we do with this? What are you really analyzing?" I took it very lightly, with great calm.

SL: You felt it had more to do with culture?

JB: I'd always kept my distance from culture — as well as from theory. I maintained a position of distrust and rejection. That's the only "radicalness" I can claim. It might have something to do with my old pataphysical training: I don't want culture; I spit on it. If a theory really becomes part of it, for me it's unspeakable. Several years ago, all that changed. Somewhere along the line I stopped living, in Canetti's sense.

SL: Something came unstuck.

JB: The giddiness I'm talking about ended up taking hold of me.

SL: A logical giddiness.

JB: Yes. I stopped working on simulation. I

felt I was going totally nuts. Finally, by various paths, all this came to have extremely direct consequences on my life. It seemed logical that something would happen, an event of this kind — but I began to wonder what theory had to do with all this. There is in theories something that does away with the feeling of being "unstuck." But what theory brings back on the other hand, to reaccentuate it, pervert it — in the full sense of the word — I'd rather not know about.

SL: *You spoke a bit earlier about the art of disappearance.*

JB: Disappearance is something completely different from death. Dying doesn't do any good. You still have to disappear. It is a mode assimilated to that of seduction. The death of meaning is not interesting in itself.

SL: *Behaviorism puts an end to meaning. It does it more radically than we do.*

JB: There meaning is truly erased, but it doesn't disappear. Pragmatism is the same as simulation pushed to the limit. Simulation puts an end to meaning absolutely, in its neutralizing, undifferentiated form. But it does it without prestige, without charm, without pleasure, without any of the effects of disappearance which are the best we can afford today.

SL: *You rediscover desire in charm. Something of desire would have to remain, otherwise...*

JB: I only resented desire in the cultural acceptance it gained. Actually desire is a term that managed to get out of the test of reality — if you'll pardon the expression — while still retaining a certain poetic density. It wasn't killed, it remains — on condition that it stays out of the libidinal.

SL: *It's desire as seduction.*

JB: In seduction, all the energy that you gathered for yourself is turned over to the object. Objective necessity occurs — an absolute surprise which takes away the effectiveness of the subject.

SL: *Exchange exerts a similar effect, but the subject's disappearance is of a statistical order. It melts into "the masses," which are conceived as an infinite commutation of individual clones — the mass as circulation, not immobility or assembly, of course.[8]*

Neutralization is a statistical fiction, a sociologist's point of view reporting the existence of a flat encephalogram on the level of culture.

JB: Well, let's be frank here. If I ever dabbled in anything in my theoretical infancy, it was philosophy more than sociology. I don't think at all in those terms. My point of view is completely metaphysical. If anything, I'm a metaphysician, perhaps a moralist, but certainly not a sociologist. The only "sociological" work I can claim is my effort to put an end to the social. to the concept of the social.[9]

SL: You proclaimed the end of the social, I guess, by contrast with another more archaic form, which Marcel Mauss defined as the "total social fact." What does that symbolic, or agonistic exchange of traditional societies mean to you now? Do you still believe it has a bearing on post-industrial societies.[10]

JB: Actually in traditional societies exchange is absent. Symbolic exchange is the opposite of exchange. The term is rather deceptive. There is an order of exchange and an order of fate. The only means of exorcising fate is through exchange; in other words, through a contractual agreement. Where exchange is not possible, fate takes over. In the case of the hostage, whenever exchange becomes impossible, you move into the order of the fatal, of the catastrophe. There is a dual reversibility, an agonistic challenge.

SL: Negotiation is no longer possible. From there on, anything can happen.

JB: I call symbolic exchange fatal: I am led to it by chance. Fate is in the dividing line separating chance and necessity, to use Jacques Monod's terms. [11]

Neither one wipes out the order of events. One — necessity — is based on an order of causes, of finality, a system of values which is that of metaphysics. The other — chance — is based on an objective by undetermined and erratic order. What I wanted to define with the "fatal" order is an objective order, but of the highest necessity. The question of finality no longer applies. An event — or a being, or a word — resolves all efforts at explanation; it imposes itself with a force which is no longer of the final or causal order. It is more final than final: it is fatal.

SL: The way speed is more mobile than movement—its pure form, independent of any destination.

JB: Yes, speed is the ecstatic form of movement. In ecstasy, there is no longer any stage — no more scene, no more theatre. But there is no more passion either. It is intense, but dispassionate. It can carry a charge of seductiveness, for seduction is an ecstatic form. The fatal is ecstasy in the form of an event, in the same way that free-floating capital is an ecstatic form of the circulation of money. They no longer bear any relationship to production.

SL: It is the extreme form of the logic of capital.

JB: The ecstatic form of capital is totally generalized exchange. An orbital form. In merchandise, money if already in process of de-referentialization. It is the transpoliticized form of merchandise. Look at what happens in the movement of money — money no longer bears any relationship to value, even in the sense in which Bataille uses the term (in order for there to be something "spent," one must still believe in value). That is what gives rise to intense miraculous effects of multiplication. The secret of gambling is that money does not exist as a value.

SL: But value returns after the fact: it's what you have to pay if you lose.

JB: Afterward, you commit suicide. But in the heat of the moment, the idea of winning or losing is relatively unimportant compared to the seductive sequence of events.

SL: Gambling is the ecstatic form of money.

JB: Gambling isn't exactly a passion: the pleasure one derives from it is too crystalline. It is a cold ecstasy which deals with money not as meaning, value, depth or substance, but in the pure form of appearance or disappearance.

SL: It's a form of imminence.

JB: Yes, but there's nothing behind it. It's the imminence of itself. Gambling is an organized catastrophic, apparitional form — a total metamorphosis.

SL: It's a game with a subject. This would explain the fascination it holds: to gamble is to forget yourself. The extreme form of neurosis — and its annulment.

JB: Gambling is a game, a challenge. There is no gambling subject: the transsubstantiation is complete. It's pure seduction. It comes from elsewhere. In theory gambling is without consequence. This is why it's so easy to condemn the "immorality" of gambling. Gambling is immoral. It bears no relation to the reality of money.

SL: It feeds on itself.

JB: It's the passion of arriving at a given object — money, in this case — and managing to completely disconnect it, to discover its means of appearing. I didn't say its means of production; we know that only too well, and it's no fun. Wherever you can find the possibility of pure appearances, you are once again in the game. It's in this sense that I no longer situate myself in the irreversible order of annihilation. The possibility of returning to a level of metamorphosis or seduction cannot be lost. There's only fate.

SL: But first this has to pass through a rage to destroy, to exterminate everything.

JB: There has to be extermination. In the final account, it's extremely rare that something can get out of the chain of cause and effect to fully appear. It is the ephemeral moment in which things take the time to appear before taking on meaning or value. What is fascinating then — what makes that moment an event — is that a mode of sociality can be created which is not the mode of exchange but occurence of pure events. The statistical occurence, on the contrary, is flat, numerical, without sequence. It is nothing but contiguity and measurement. We live in a world that is very loose, quite lax, in which things are more or less arbitrary, disconnected and therefore sporadic, erratic. The order of the fatal, on the other hand, is the site of symbolic exchange. There is no more liberty, everything is locked in a sequential chain.

SL: *That was already the case with the primitive ceremonial.*

JB: I don't exclude rituals and ceremonies. Whatever reaches the level of pure appearance — a person, an event, an act — enters the realm of the fatal. It cannot be deciphered or interpreted. The subject has nothing to say about it. Events emerge from any and every place, but from an absolute beyond, with that true strangeness which alone is fascinating. It belongs neither to the order of the normal nor to the accidental. It is a necessity greater than the law, something like objective chance without any effect of the unconscious, whose fate would be repressed.

SL: *A successful event leaves nothing behind it.*

JB: In the finalities that one can assign oneself, values are always relative. They must be invested. They are necessary, but subjectively. For example, the fetishistic object topples the subject's need to place itself in the transcendental center of the world. On the contrary, at any given moment the universe has the possibility of incarnating itself in a detail which is unjustifiable in its own right. The universal no longer exists, there is nothing left but a singularity which can take on the aspect of totality.

SL: *Singularities, in the Hegelian sense, have a particularity and a universal aspect. They are moments.*

JB: Yes, whereas now singularities very likely no longer have any universal becoming. The universal is a game preserve, it is the site of that indifferent strategy. It cannot be assigned an end, a reason, a meaning. It is total crystallization around an event.

SL: *Deleuze dealt with this problematic in* Logique du Sens (Logic of Meaning).[12] *But for him, the logic of appearances, the play of surfaces does not abolish subjectivity.*

JB: For me events are no longer those of the subject; they reach a point where they function all by themselves. It is a pure connection of events in a logic of appearances, if you like, which meets seduction. The order of seductive connections stands in opposition to rational connections, whatever they may be, and also to delirious connections, and possibly to molecular ones. It is not an order of the accidental; an accident does not fascinate me in that sense. The catastrophe does not fascinate me as an accident, it fascinates me as a necessity. That appearances function all by themselves is based on a necessity much more implacable than the chain of causes which is for its part relatively arbitrary, as is the connection of the signifier and the signified. The connection, the chain of appearances are signs that do not, in fact, make sense. There is a rule to the game.

Chapter Three

Law and Rules — Crisis, Catastrophe —
Poetry — A Sign is as Good as the Thing Itself —
Femininity, Childhood — "Strategy" of the
Fatal — The Principle of Evil — Model and
Truth — Beyond Esthetic Judgement —
Fashion, Politics — The Ecstacy of Forms —
The Media Doesn't Mystify — Beau Brummel —
Power/Knowledge/Will — Revolution,
Devolution — May '68, an Inconsequential
Event.

SL: Is the fatal the fulfillment of an empty rule?
JB: A rule can be perfectly arbitrary in its
enunciation, but it is much more unbreakable
than the "law," which can be transgressed. You
can do anything with the law. With the rule, on
the other hand, either you play or you don't
play. If you play, the rule is implacable. You
can't get around it. It would be idiotic to
transgress it. The rule of the game — the

seductive sequence — is played in an extremely ceremonialized fashion. Situations can be replayed indefinitely, the "rule" does not change. But it is secret, never known, never spoken. If it were known, things would become visible and reversible again. With causal or rational sequences, you have crisis. With seductive sequences, on the contrary, you are — literally — in a catastrophic order.

SL: That's the logic of the avalanche.

JB: Forms that are beyond judgment have a much greater power of fascination, but they are for that same reason terribly dangerous for any order whatsoever. They can no longer be controlled. At any given moment a category or a form stops representing itself, it no longer enters the stage of representation, it no longer functions according to its end. It doubles back upon itself, taking a curve so rapid that it reaches a kind of potentialization. All the rest goes into a state of weightlessness. In the language of poetry we are familiar with those sequences in which things seem to take place without continuity, without consequence, without mediation. Language is always an order of seduction to the extent that it is a mutant order. If you suppose continuous, progressive, linear order then it is still based on a mutational "superstructure." The words in a poem are of that order. They do not go through the meaning. One word calls forth another in a catastrophe of charm. One leads to another in a thoughtless, unintelligible way. I am not seeking the irrational. On the contrary, we know that there is a necessity without its being transcendental or providential. The same thing can take place in the order of facts, of actions, of existential situations.

SL: *It is ritual without the sacred, the tragic without the tragedy.*

JB: It is not a sacred universe, even though there is indeed a tragic aspect in seduction. If you accept the rule of the game, you can never know in advance to what degree of concatenation of appearances a strategy may lead. Take, for example, the story of the woman to whom a man sends an ardent love letter. She asks him what part of her seduced him the most. What else can he answer? Her eyes, of course. And he receives in the mail, wrapped in brown paper, the woman's eye. The man is shattered, destroyed. The woman sets herself as the destiny of the other. Literalizing the metaphor, she abolishes the symbolic order. The sign becomes the thing. The subject is caught in the trap of his own desire. She loses an eye, he loses face.

SL: In De la Seduction (On Seduction) you took another metaphor literally, that of the woman-object.[13] *It meant (in appearance at least) taking feminism against the grain, with, I believe, unexpected potentializations.*

JB: I consider woman the absence of desire. It is of little import whether or not that corresponds to real women. It is my conception of "femininity."

SL: Isn't it surprising that in the midst of metamorphoses, the feminine figure for you remains fixed. That's very nostalgic, that polarity of roles.

JB: But I don't believe in it. For me, femininity is non-polar. Contrary to masculinity, woman has no anxious focalization on sex, she can transform herself into herself.

SL: That means becoming-woman is something that can occur in women or in men.

JB: Of course. Femininity appears in certain individuals, men or women. But woman is the object which plays out all the liquidities of desire. The drama of love is entirely in men, that of charm completely in women.

SL: Speaking of love, you replace intersubjectivity with a reciprocal transformation. A passage into the other, but an other which is no longer there.

JB: That is the problem of otherness. As in the world, or on the terrain of sex, no one is the other of the other sex any longer. It is not narcissism, which is a concretion accomplished in solitude; not otherness either. Each one functions within his / her own nebula, accomplishing his / her own virtuality.

SL: If I understand, the process of becoming-woman common to both sexes is the accomplishment of each one as a separate object. Their reciprocal challenge is to become more woman than woman, in a word, to attain that femininity which each one can attain only in relationship to himself / herself.

JB: I think here of the strategic position of the process of becoming- object. What interests me now is no longer the subject but the object and its destiny. You become the destiny of the other. It is clearer when you think of childhood. The child always has a double strategy. He has the possibility of offering himself as object, protected, recognized, destined as a child to the pedagogical function; and at the same time he is fighting on equal terms. At some level the child knows that he is not a child, but the adult does not know that. That is the secret.

SL: *That's what is fueling the hysterical campaign against "child abuse." Adults panic in the face of the extermination of childhood, which they on the other hand are encouraging. Childhood constitutes the last anchor of our culture. If childhood is lost, what is morality to be based on? The social repression of "child molesters" is all the more ferocious.*[14]

JB: The problem is that everything has been unleashed on childhood. There has been quite a "palingenesis" on childhood, no psychoanalytic joke intended; now there it has been taken seriously. The category of childhood is defined historically, and there psychology begins: child psychology, therapy, pedagogy, it all follows. If, going against every assumption, you maintain the little utopian fact that childhood does not exist and that the child is perhaps the only one to know it, then everything blows up in your face. That is what I was trying to say about women. Women, children, animals — we must not be afraid of assimilations — do not just have a subject-consciousness, they have a kind of objective ironic presentiment that the category into which they have been placed does not exist. Which allows them at any given moment to make use of a double strategy. It isn't psychology, it's strategy.

SL: When you speak of the strategy of the fatal, what interests me most is the strategy. What is to be done?

JB: No, it's completely antinomical. It's not really strategy. That's a play on words to dramatize the total passage from the subject to the object. Whether you call it the revenge of the object, or the Evil Genius of matter, it is not representable. But it is a power all the same. In fact, I would go along with calling it the principle of Evil, of irreconciliation, the way the Good is the principle of reconciliation. That exists, it is inextricable, it cannot be destroyed.

SL: Can you still invoke a strategy to account for situations in which the subject has no place?

JB: Only an "objective" strategy that no one could recognize. What I foresee is a transposition of all forms and the impossibility of any politics. There is something like a threshold of inertia. Beyond that, forms snowball, terror is unleashed as an empty form.

SL: Panic.

JB: Right. It's the other form of the ecstatic, its catastrophic form, in the almost neutral sense of the term, in its mathematical extension. It is a completely alien response of the object world to the subject world, of a completely external destiny which occurs with an absolute surprise and whose symbolic wave strikes the human world.

SL: You see several sides to ecstasy?

JB: I see two. Take a model. Its ecstatic side is to be truer than the truth; it creates a kind of giddiness, a kind of inflation of truth. A model is a rather pathetic thing. But take fashion for example. Fashion participates in this phenomenon absolutely. It doesn't depend on any sort of esthetic judgment. It's not the beautiful opposed to the ugly, it's what's more beautiful than the beautiful. The obese — that famous fat American — is not opposed to the skinny one. He is fatter than fat, and that is fascinating. Fashion is the absolute formalization of the beautiful. It functions by means of the unconditional transmutation of forms. Ecstatic forms can be static and cold; sometimes they can be more enchanting, warmer. There is a splendor of fashion, and, behind it, an uncontrollable rule of the game. A rule which conveys the objective irony of fashion. Everything that can be invented deliberately falls flat on its face, and it's something else that catches on instead.

SL: Can fashion serve as a model for politics?

JB: Fashion has always been at odds with politics and scorned by politics. But you cannot politically oppose fashion to politics. Fashion is a spendid form of metamorphosis. It is both a ritual and a ceremony. It can't be programmed.

SL: Could happy, ecstatic political forms be conceived of?

JB: It's rather difficult to sort out happy and unhappy forms. Seduction, like fashion, is a happy form, beyond the beauty of desire: "I am not beautiful, I am worse." Seduction uses signs which are already simulators to make them into the falser than false. It displaces them, turns them into traps and produces a splendid effect snatched from the imperative of veracity of signs, and even of desire, which is no longer at stake.

SL: Must all political rituals necessarily be programmed?

JB: Politics functioned in terms of distinctive oppositions: the left or the right. As in other areas you have the true or the false, the beautiful or the ugly, etc. Now, at a given point the energy of a situation stopped depending on this kind of dissociation. It is no longer the dialectic of the two terms that organizes things, but the fact that the forms each go their separate ways, meaninglessly, senselessly. It is the truer than true, or the falser than false. A form shoots off in a kind of relentless logic, uncalculated, without any history, without any memory, the way cancer cells go off in an organic direction. That logic seems to me more interesting because it does after all correspond more to the way things are evolving nowadays.

SL: Where do you see that logic at work in the political field right now? In the media?

JB: The media are supposed to be a fabulous distortion. But behind that analysis still lurks a symbolic demand for truth. Where does that distortion come from? Placing the media in the system of will— choice— liberty is really hopeless. All you can do is invoke a total alienation of the political subject, accuse the power structure of manipulating, etc. The power structure doesn't manipulate TV, it functions exactly the way it does. It relies on representations, it also secrets them with the scant political relief of a TV image, without accuracy or energy, to the point of merging with the civil society in the indistinction of the political scene. Meaning manages to disappear in the horizon of communication. The media are simply the locus of this disappearance, which is always a challenge to the powers that be. It's becoming urgent to reformulate a theory of the media as "agents provocateurs" of information overload, turning political debate into a gigantic abyss. Let's get rid of the notion that the media mystify and ailenate. We've had enough of that.

SL: The theory of alienation has become the echo necessary to the media for their existence. It amounts indirectly to giving them the benefit of an intention. They don't deserve that.

JB: You're right. In the transpolitical, there is no more who. Then if it isn't the power structure, which seems pretty clear, if there is no longer a subject, is there a strategy of the object, objective irony?

SL: The media industry never does anything but reproduce its own necessity. As William Burroughs

*said: all things considered, the public could get along
very well without the news.*

JB: There you have it. All that is done now is
to display a range of choices which are all equally
potential or fulfilled. Have you heard this story
about Beau Brummel? He traveled a great deal,
always in the company of his manservant. One
day he was in Scotland, in a region where there
are many lakes, each one more beautiful than the
other. Brummel turned to his servant and asked
him, "Which lake do I prefer?" Having to
choose is really a bore. That's what servants are
for. In any case, that's not what counts. Power —
Knowledge — Will — let the inventors of those
ideas take responsibility for them. It makes
perfect sense to me that the great masses, very
snobbishly, delegate to the class of intellectuals,
of politicians, this business of managing, of
choosing, of knowing what one wants. They are
joyously dumping all those burdensome
categories that no one, deep down inside, really
wants any part of. That people want to be told
what they want is certainly not true; it is not
clear either that they really want to know what
they want, or that they desire to want at all. The
whole edifice of socialism is based on that

assumption. They start from the fact that this is what people ought to want, that they are social in the sense that they are supposed to know themselves, know what they want. I think we have pressed beyond that point, beyond truth, beyond reality.

SL: Objective irony, that would be the masses' offhand way of getting rid of their responsibilities, turning power back to its fantasies, knowledge to its obsessions, will to its illusions. The silent majority, as you see it then, is not the accomplice of law and order, but rather its silence is a dead silence. The masses are playing dead. And this stubborn silence, this insolent reserve, would sanction the disappearance of the social.

JB: Exactly. The large systems of information relieve the masses of the responsibility of having to know, to understand, to be informed, to be up on things. Advertising relieves people of the responsibility of having to choose, which is perfectly human and perfectly horrible. As for power, it has always seemed ironic to me to delegate it to someone. That's like catching him in a trap, and that trap closes on the political class itself. I see all of this as a profound reversal of strategy on the part of the masses. They are no longer involved in a process of subversion or revolution, but in some gigantic devolution from an unwanted liberty — with some evil genius lurking behind it all. I think we are beginning to realize how much terror lies at the heart of the paradise of communication. Beyond that, events are inconsequential, and that is even more true for theories.

SL: But there is power in the fact of being inconsequential.

JB: That was what interested me about May '68. Behind the political, revolutionary, and historical scene, and also behind the failure, there was the power of an event which managed to absorb its own continuity. It makes it implode, succeeds in swallowing its own energy and disappearing.

SL: May '68 swept down on France like an avalanche, and no sooner had it appeared than it disappeared, mysteriously, practically without a trace.

JB: Then where has all that energy gone? Nowhere — certainly not into socialism in any case. It must have been reabsorbed somewhere — without necessarily remaining underground so as to emerge later. For me May '68 was the first event that corresponded to this inertial point of the political scene. Continuity disappears. Only such things are fascinating.

Chapter Four

Going to Extremes — The Scenario of
Deterrence — Terrorism and Hyperreality —
The Impossible War — Fascism and Trans-
politics — May '68 — Two Forms of Secret —
The Ecstasy of Socialism — The Story of Sophie
Calle — Ends, Means — Power Doesn't Exist —
God's Strategy — Italy in Political Simulation —
The Challenge to the Social

SL: *Comprehension is no longer involved there.*

JB: No. But more comprehension is going to
be re-secreted. It is intolerable for everybody
that events should be inconsequential, or that
their own desires should be inconsequential.
And, in the last analysis, that theory should be
inconsequential. No exceptions allowed.

SL: *All of that is part of what Paul Virilio calls
" the esthetic of disappearance."*[15]

JB: From time to time theory allows itself

beautiful effects of disappearance. What more can one do? In terms of results there is no difference between what came to an end with May '68 and whatever Giscard d'Estaing or Mitterand accomplished. Acceleration permits another kind of disappearance effect, another order that can't be reached in any other way. Therefore, I agree with Paul Virilio on the idea of theory going to extremes. You will ask me, why are people going to those extremes, if you don't suppose that at some point the world, and the universe, too, is in the grips of a movement to extremes. There you are, apparently, forced to make an almost objective, rational hypothesis. It is impossible to think that theory can be nothing more than fiction. Otherwise no one would bother producing theory any more. You have to believe that going somewhere is not just a metaphor. And then, if it is a challenge, in any case there is a partner. It is no longer a dialectic, but there is a rule of the game. Somewhere there must be a limit that constitutes the real in order for there to be theory. A point where things can stick, or from which they can take off.

SL: *For Virilio there is definitely a trend toward*

extremes at work in the world today: the military class is swallowing up civilian society before disappearing itself in a suicidal race.[16]

JB: Virilio's calculation is to push the military to a kind of extreme absolute of power, which can only ultimately cause its own downfall, place it before the judgment of God and absorb it into the society it destroys. Virilio carries out this calculation with such an identification or obsession that I can only credit him at times with a powerful sense of irony: the system devours its own principle of reality, inflates its own empty forms until it reaches an absolute and its own ironic destiny of reversal. I myself am not so interested in military hardware, but in software. It's the form of his idea that strikes me as valid.

SL: The state of emergency, the risk of nuclear extermination — you can dismiss all that?

JB: Why, of course I think about it, but for me there is no fatal term. The nuclear threat is part of a "soft" mode of extermination, bit by bit, by deterrence, not at all an apocalyptic term. It is the scenario of deterrence that Paul Virilio shares with me, apparently, because he moves back and forth between the real term and the mythical term, which is mine. For me, it's in the realm of the intellectual wager. If there were an absolute term of the nuclear apocalypse in the realm of the real, then at that point I would stop, I wouldn't write anymore! God knows, if the metaphor really collapses into reality, I won't have any more to do. That would not even be a question of resignation — it's no longer possible to think at that point.

SL: The implosive side of the nuclear threat paralyzes everything. It's more than deterrence, it's political tetanus.

JB: Virilio is very interested in strategic vicissitudes; I don't have the patience. Does the nuclear threat have a political term? Or does it make it disappear when the bomb hits the ground? It's the same as for the media, I no longer attach any importance to it. Can there be a political management of a material that is "transpolitical?" I don't see where it could come from.

SL: Let's go back to your analysis of terrorism, which led you to discard the concept of the social. For a number of years we witnessed a trend toward extremes in the confrontation between the Red Army Faction and the German government. Now what was the final outcome? A challenge; implosive forms of confrontation? Not at all. Once the extremes were eliminated (Stammheim), the possibility was established of bargaining, of striking a compromise. Politics regained the upper hand, and history with it.

JB: Terrorism can have a visible, a spectacular form. It is still part of the dramatic, practically, in the historical realm. So it can be succeeded by a kind of negotiable terror. The term "hostage," as I have used it, would then qualify not only the visible dramas of the taking of hostages, but rather the hyperreality of everyday life which is situated well beyond negotiable terror. It's the same as for deterrence. It's not the actual terror of the orbitting bombs' power of destruction; Virilio says that very clearly. War having also become an impossible exchange, the hostage would only qualify a situation in which all exchange has become impossible.

SL: *War is perhaps impossible: it continues nonetheless everywhere you look.*

JB: People get killed, people die in war, of course. But it would still involve a kind of conspiracy to set up a *trompe l'oeil* decor, the way city planners make provisions for parks and greenery. The history of Europe is perhaps of that order — an effort to circumscribe Europe as a space of freedom, a political space, etc., to escape that panic of the insolubility, the impossibility of a declared war, of a war which can really signify itself. It is set up as a war space in an attempt to somehow alter, however minimally, the situation of generalized dissuasion, which is intolerable. The consequences are felt at some point with this blockage, this leukemia of political life which is unbearable for everybody, for the ruling classes as well as for those who are ruled. But at this point war certainly no longer has the same meaning, nor does art, or politics, or the hostage. Everything takes on another existence, with different stakes.

SL: You once tried, along with Virilio, to theorize the concept of the "transpolitical?" Is the transpolitical situated on the other side of the political logic of consequences? Can that be a way of saving the political?

JB: The efforts to save it, that is what we are witnessing all around us. Those efforts are occupying the scene. The present, or recent, form of socialism in France — I call it "ecstatic" — in that sense it is transpolitical. It proceeds from a model. Socialism realizes, hyperrealizes a model which no longer has any veracity or original passion.

SL: The transpolitical would be a negative notion then. It's the same scene but emptied out from within.

JB: In that sense, yes. That is part of the exterminating analysis. I'm not crazy about the term itself. It's almost too "figurative." It signifies that there could still be a beyond, and that we ought to go and take a look at what's going on there. I prefer the formulation in terms of that point Canetti describes. We don't know what happened after that. The traditional points of reference are no longer usable, but we don't know what we are in. To demand a degree of truth is always problematical. Fascism was already something like that. It was a kind of potentialization. That is why it remains relatively inexplicable in political terms, such as capitalism or class struggle.

SL: There is a secret to fascism.

JB: Yes. It derives its overwhelming necessity precisely from its being isolated and disconnected, as in the case of the catastrophe, but this necessity is far beyond any rational finality. The secret lies in that total autonomy of a narrative, of a form, a myth that can no longer be described in a logical, coherent and acceptable manner, but runs amok. Past a certain threshold of inertia, forms start snowballing, stampeding, and terror is unleashed as an empty form. There comes about a swept-away effect, an effect that feeds on itself and can become the source of immense energies, as fascism did, unfortunately. When effects go faster than causes, they devour them. I could easily see the "speed-up" analyzed by Virilio from this angle, as an attempt to accelerate faster than linearity can. Movement goes somewhere, speed goes nowhere. May '68 was an illogical event, irreducible to simulation, one which had no status other than that of coming from someplace else — a kind of pure object or event. Its strangeness derives from a logic of our own system, but not from its history. It is a prodigious effect, and it is situated on the other side of that crucial point Canetti describes and that I mentioned earlier.

SL: *The cause of an event is always imagined after the fact. After that jolly May, we were treated to the curious spectacle of causes racing after effects.*

JB: May '68 is an event which it has been impossible to rationalize or exploit, from which nothing has been concluded. It remains indecipherable. It was the forerunner of nothing.

SL: *There are no children of May.*

JB: Perhaps a kind of "secret" is involved here too.

SL: *Tell me about secrets.*

JB: There are fundamentally two kinds of secrets. The obscene form of the secret involves a saturation of the event with explanations. The other kind involves something which is not hidden and therefore cannot be expressed directly in words. It is this second kind of secret which makes the event somehow innocent. Now what can you do with that? Ordinarily, when things happen, you pick them up as best you can as a subject. In the case of May '68, we have been forced to give all our subjective energy to the object.

SL: *The event becomes a kind of slippery object that refers each subject back to his/her own fantasies without ever allowing itself to be touched. There are no children of May.*

JB: That event disappeared without leaving a trace behind it other than this secondary and parodic effect, this second or thirdhand product manufactured to occupy a political scene that has been utterly absorbed and destroyed: French socialism.

SL: The socialists' error is to have occupied the vacuum and to have allowed themselves to be sucked into the black hole of politics.

JB: There are two ways of seeing this. You can say there used to be a political sphere and there isn't anymore, following a Foucauldian genealogy. That was how Foucault talked about man. There is no longer a scene of politics the way it was organized around the history of power relations, production, classes. Power is no longer an objective, locatable process. This is what I say is lost, if we can speak of an end of something. We are elsewhere. If, on the contrary, the political sphere consists in knowing how to play on an event or a thing on the basis of its objective or conscious end — but in order to ward it off — then power, in political terms, becomes a kind of challenge.

SL: A challenge from the powers that be not to exercise power?

JB: I wonder, in fact, if true power, the power that deepens the meaning of politics, is not the one that pulls back from itself, that plays out its own death, without even willing it consciously. The secret of power is that it can no longer be occupied, no longer be taken. When "power" is confused with the "power structure," you know it is no longer power. It becomes extremely vulnerable.

SL: Could we not conceive this phenomenon in a more active fashion? The political as the art of not occupying a position yourself, but creating a void for others to rush into it.

JB: The political sphere must keep secret the rule of the game that, in reality, power doesn't exist. Its strategy is, in fact, always creating a space of optical illusion, maintaining itself in total ambiguity, total duplicity in order to throw the others into this space. This is Machiavelli's strategy.

SL: It is also the story of Sophie Calle.[17]

JB: Right. For no particular reason, as you know, she followed a stranger in the street; she became his shadow and thus, in a certain sense, erased his traces, acted as his destiny. Creating a void, she asked the other to fill it. She herself is nothing. She has no desire of her own in all this. She doesn't want to go anywhere, even though she follows him all the way to Venice. She doesn't want to find out what he is or to know his life. She is the proof that, although he thought he was going somewhere, in fact he is going nowhere. Where he supposedly is, there's no one. We could envision this story in terms of Balthazar Gracian. Is God's strategy really to lead man to his own ends, in other words to move man closer to the image of God according to a progressive- evolutionary process? God isn't so dumb, Gracian says. Nowhere does it say that man wants to arrive at his own end, which would be the idea of God in its canonical form. God's strategy is much more subtle, which no doubt corresponds to man's desire not to give a shit about his own end. God's strategy — that of all the Jesuit manuals that were incredibly widespread in the seventeenth century — is to keep man in an eternal suspense. And that is in the order of politics. Which reveals God as being fairly malicious, perverse, given man's faculty to erect almost anything as a finality. Any possible illusion to avoid the last judgment, which is truly Hell. In fact, politics is always in a contrary, twisted, or simply "seductive" relation to its own ends. God is much more interested in the game, in the possibility of playing with ends, even using means. Furthermore, this proposition — the end and the means — has always favored the ends at the expense of the means. Since the means are immoral, the ends must be moral. But we could very well turn the proposition around, and this is precisely what the Jesuits do: play with the means, whatever, for the ends cannot be found anymore. For the Jesuits — and this is their basic proposition — it is impossible to establish a proof of God's existence. So all right, God exists, the grace of God exists, but it has nothing to do with us because what we're dealing with is a strategic worldliness. And with this you can play. There are only means.

SL: In Simulations, what especially interested me, in fact, was the possibility of effecting this kind of diversion. I was struck by the fact that the Italians — in particular certain figures of the Autonomia movement[18] — when confronted with an emergency situation, found in certain of your propositions, even if they were disenchanted ones, instruments that they immediately tried to use politically. Instead of respecting your own ends (or their absence as ends ...), they took certain of your concepts as floating theoretical tools capable of being reinvested in

*particular situations. In short, they diverted your own
diversion. I admit that I like this practical perversion
of your own theoretical perversion.*

JB: That indeed seems to me to be the
situation in Italy. Everyone seems to be party to
prolonging a situation that isn't exactly
political — in any case, no one can pull the
strings anymore. The situation is seductive
because of that kind of indecisiveness with
which everyone plays without necessarily being
aware of it. I like that Italian ability to turn
around, turn away an objective state that would
otherwise be catastrophic: the State could have
disappeared a long time ago, along with politics.

SL: In fact, the State has never existed there...

JB: I think that every other country is in the
same situation, despite appearances to the
contrary. They are all in a situation of political
simulation, but on the sly. Italy, on the other
hand, seems to be exercising the simulacrum as
such, seduction as such.

*SL: The simulacrum supports politics, instead of
wiping it out.*

JB: The Italians have a long tradition of all this
with the Jesuits and the Church — in the way
Nietzsche meant. For them, the end is always

imminent, but at the same time there is a possibility of almost joyful resurrection with each event, and that is phenomenal. We certainly couldn't say the same of Poland ... who are ideologically active cannot help fantasizing about a world that would make more sense, or that would return to sense. And so you get to terrorism, which is an enormous fantasy of a political order of the State the better to murder it, to massacre it. But what game is terrorism playing? Terrorism makes no more sense than the State does. They are accomplices in a circular set-up.

SL: In Germany as in Italy (neither country ever having been unified or centralized), terrorism helps the State appear.

JB: It's the role of a partner more than of an adversary. It's always like that: events are played out on a conscious level of adversity, of war, of irreconcilable, incompatible ideologies, but in reality what's happening underneath it all? Who would dream that the situation can become so totally terroristic that in fact it joins its other extreme? I don't see how all this can end. It is not objectively representable.

SL: You see in the terrorist act, as in nuclear confrontation between the Great Powers (which is, in fact, State terrorism), not an explosive phenomenon, but the point at which the social implodes. But what is "the social?" You hypostatize a complex reality in an abstraction, only to immediately send the abstraction back to the domain of unreality and proclaim its end. Isn't that a bit too easy?

JB: But I take the social as already hypostatized. From hypostasis to ecstasy!

SL: If the social doesn't exist — if it has never existed outside of the theoretical imagination — then it can't implode.

JB: All right, that's entirely plausible. And yet you could also state the hypothesis that at a given moment the social did exist, but not at all as a representation of society, nor in a positive sense, but rather as a challenge to the reality of things, as a virulent myth. This is how Georges Bataille saw sociology: as a challenge to the very nature of the social and to society. History also existed in that sense. But then, that's not really existence, because when history begins to exist, very quickly there's nothing left but to treat it as an instance of jurisdiction and meaning. I have never resolved that ambiguity between being and existence; I believe it's insoluble.

Chapter Five

The Challenge to the Real— A Geoseismic
View of Things — Theory as Event — The Art of
Disappearance— The Vortex of Implosion—
Seduction— The Malice of the Social— The
Slipperiness of Forms— The Evil Genius of
Theory— Extermination— Metaphysics and
Metatheory— "Forgetting" Theory— Myth
and Serials— The Media's Anti-Destiny

SL: *For Nietzsche, the philosopher must decipher
action. He must actively evaluate the forces
confronting each other in society. You conceive of the
social as the depletion of an empty form. What role,
then, do you attribute to theory? Must it be a virulent
myth, as it is for Bataille? But if the social has
become weightless, what does myth attack? And for
what cause?*

JB: I admit, that question of theory troubles
me. Where is theory situated today? Is it
completely satellized? Is it wandering in realms

which no longer have anything to do with real facts? What is analysis? As long as you consider that there is a real world, then by the same token there is a possible position for theory. Let us say a dialectical position, for the sake of argument. Theory and reality can still be exchanged at some point — and that is ideality. There is after all a point of contact between the two. And then you can transform the world, and theory does transform the world. That is not at all my position anymore. Moreover, it never was. But I have never succeeded in formulating it. In my opinion, theory is simply a challenge to the real. A challenge to the world to exist. Very often a challenge to God to exist. But there is more than theory. In the beginning, religion, in its former heretical phase, was always a negation — at times a violent one — of the real world, and this is what gave it strength. After that, religion became a process of reconciliation rather than a pleasure or reality principle. This can hold true for theory as well: a theory can attempt to reconcile the real with theory itself. And then there is a principle of antagonism — an absolutely irreconcilable, almost Manichaean antagonism. You maintain a position of challenge, which is different from unreality.

SL: Still, isn't that exactly what you do: make stakes unreal by pushing them to the limit?

JB: But I hold no position on reality. Reality remains an unshakeable postulate toward which you can maintain a relation either of adversity or of reconciliation. The real— all things considered, perhaps it exists— no, it doesn't exist— is the insurmountable limit of theory. The real is not an objective status of things, it is the point at which theory can do nothing. That does not necessarily make of theory a failure. The real is actually a challenge to the theoretical edifice. But in my opinion theory can have no status other than that of challenging the real. At that point, theory is no longer theory, it is the event itself. There is no "reality" with respect to which theory could become dissident or heretical, pursuing its fate other than in the objectivity of things. Rather, it's the objectivity of things we must question. What is this objectivity? In the so-called "real world," don't things always happen that way? By a divergence, a trajectory, a curve which is not at all the linear curve of evolution? We could perhaps develop a model of drifting plates, to speak in seismic terms, in the theory of catastrophes. The seismic is our form of the slipping and sliding of the referential. The end of the infrastructure. Nothing remains but shifting movements that provoke very powerful raw events. We no longer take events as revolutions or effects of the superstructure, but as underground effects of skidding, fractal zones in which things happen. Between the plates, continents do not quite fit together, they slip under and over each other. There is no more system of reference to tell us what happened to the geography of things. We can only take a geoseismic view. Perhaps this is also true in the construction of a society, a mentality, a value-system. Things no longer meet head-on; they slip past one another. Everyone claims to "be in reality." But the test of reality is not decisive. Nothing happens in the real.

SL: Is anything happening in the theory then?

JB: Theory dismantles the reality principle; it's not at all a means of objectivizing things in order to transform them. No, I don't believe that. At a certain point I felt — if we suppose that the real, and social practices, are indeed there — that I was launched on a trajectory that was increasingly diverging, becoming asymptotic. It would be an error to constantly try to catch hold of that zig-zagging line of reality. The only thing you can do is let it run all the way to the end. At that point they can raise any objection they like about the relation to reality: we are in a totally arbitrary situation, but there is an undeniable internal necessity. From that point on, theory maintains absolutely no relation with anything at all; it becomes an event in and of itself. We can no longer fix the way things are going.

SL: I wonder if there isn't a kind of "skidding" endemic to theory. When theory manages to complete itself, following its internal logic, that's when it disappears. Its accomplishment is its abolition.

JB: Yes, I really believe that's true. Can theory (I'm speaking here about what I've done) produce, not a model, but a utopian, metaphorical representation of an event, even as its entire cyclical trajectory is being accomplished, completed? I think there is a destiny of theory. There is a curve we can't escape. You know that my way is to make ideas appear, but as soon as they appear I immediately try to make them disappear. That's what the game has always consisted of. Strictly speaking, nothing remains but a sense of dizziness, with which you can't do anything.

SL: Isn't that a little bit suicidal?

JB: It's suicidal, but in a good way. If this game didn't exist, there would be no pleasure in writing, or in theorizing.

SL: Theory, or the pleasure of disappearing...

JB: There is an art of disappearing, a way of modulating it and making it into a state of grace. This is what I'm trying to master in theory.

SL: It's the end of theory, at least in Canetti's sense.

JB: Yes, in that sense.

SL: Theory implodes.

JB: It's possible that theory will implode, that it will absorb its own meaning, that it will end up at best mastering its disappearance. But it doesn't happen like that. We must manage to choke back the meanings we produce — which always tend to be produced. If a theory — or a poem, or any other kind of writing (it's not endemic to theory) — indeed manages to implode, to constitute a concentric vortex of implosion, then there are no other effects of meaning. Theory has an immediate effect — a very material one as well — of being a void. It's not so easy to create a void. And besides, there's catastrophe all around it. I don't see how theory and reality can go together. Can we implode in the real with charm? Without going all the way to suicide, we continually play on the process of disappearance in our relations to others. Not by making ourselves scarce, but by challenging the other to make us reappear. That's what seduction is, in the good sense. Not a process of expansion and conquest, but the implosive process of the game.

SL: You theorize the way others go to a casino. It's your gambling side; you swoop down on a theoretical object — Foucault, for example — with a cold passion and you totally disconnect it from its own thrust...

JB: There has to be some pleasure at stake, of course, which is neither the pleasure of prophecy nor, I think, of annihilation (destruction for destruction's sake). A perverse pleasure, in short. Theory must be played the way we said gambling was before.

SL: The secret of gambling is that money doesn't exist. Does theory? have a secret too?

JB: The secret of theory is that truth doesn't

exist. You can't confront it in any way. The only thing you can do is play with some kind of provocative logic. Truth constitutes a space that can no longer be occupied. The whole strategy is, indeed, not to occupy it, but to work around it so that others come to occupy it. It means creating a void so that others will fall into it.

SL: If theory can no longer occupy anything, can it at least constitute a challenge to the system to bring about its own annihilation?

JB: I have my doubts about its capacities in that respect. Those in power manage it much better than we could. The French socialists were wiped out because they couldn't see the malice of the social, which the Jesuits know so well. They should have had a more sporting idea of struggle: the slipperiness of forms. By trying to establish stability the socialists lost every time. They were always completely out of step with their system of cultural projection. The ground they fell on was quicksand. So what else could they do? What position can theory hold when it comes to thinking up events of that order? In concrete terms, I can't see any. Except perhaps in the twisting in which systems, in the simulated references they latch onto (the masses, the media), end up turning on themselves without intending to, and skidding. To me this seems pure genius, in the evil sense. It's a hypothesis, but a rather effective one.

SL: Theory can anticipate or hasten the catastrophic aspect of things.

JB: We could say that theory is ahead of the state of things, that it moves too fast and thus is in a position of destiny with respect to what could happen. In reality, things happen in such a way that they are always absolutely ahead of us, as Rilke said. We're always late, and therefore they are always unpredictable. No matter how, things are always much further along than theory simply by virtue of the fact that the use of discourse is in the domain of metaphor. We can't escape it. In language we are condemned to using ambiguous extrapolations. If we claim a truth, we push effects of meaning to the extreme within a model. All that theory can do is be rigourous enough to cut itself off from any system of reference, so that it will at least be current, on the scale of what it wishes to describe.

SL: You've cut yourself off from every system of reference, but not from referentiality. What I see you describing is not a challenge to the real, but a challenge internal to theory. You don't criticize the genealogical attitude or the libidinal position, you send them spinning away like tops. You wholly embrace the movement that animates them, you amplify their concepts to the maximum, pulling them into the vortex of your own dizziness. You draw them into an endless spiral which, like the treatment of myths by Levi-Strauss, leads them bit by bit to their own exhaustion.

JB: That's right. Thus theory is exterminated. It no longer has any term, literally. You can't find an end for it anymore. That's one mode of disappearance.

SL: By pushing theory to its limit the way you do, you are hyper-realizing it. You take away from theory its substance, to exhaust it, to extenuate it in its form, and then you "forget it" as a body in suspension might be left behind. You don't even simulate the real, you play God's advocate, the evil genius of theory. More Foucaldian than Foucault, you evaporate his microphysics; more schizo than Deleuze and Guattari, you straddle their fluxes, denying them any resting point. You are not the metaphysician you would like people to take you for; you are a metatheoretician. A simulator of theory.

No wonder theoreticians accuse you of being an agent provocateur. You aren't theoretical, you are "worse". You put theory into a state of grace into which you dare the world to follow you.

JB: Theory is simulation. At least that is the usage of it I have. Both simulation and challenge. It isn't deliberate. It started that way, that's all. I don't want to give it a general form.

SL: *You catch concepts in their own trap — that is, in yours — abolishing every certainty by dint of fidelity. That is the position of humor, which can be sad, as well as tongue-in-cheek. You adopt the imperceptible insolence of the servant challenging his master (his intellectual masters) to take him seriously. Calling your bluff would mean getting entangled in your game. But to evade your challenge still amounts to lending you a hand. You "forget" those whom you vampirize, but you never allow yourself to be forgotten. You are like the media, about which one can say nothing without oneself becoming implicated in it. What allows you to understand it so well, is that you are included in it. You are both playing the same game. You both use the same strategy. You don't speak about the media, the media speaks through you. As soon as you turn on your theoretical screen, the great myths of history are turned into a soap opera, or into "serials." You make them share the fate of that TV program, "Holocaust," which you analyzed so well.*[19]

JB: I don't deny history. It's an immense toy.

SL: Yes, if you remain glued to the screen, or fascinated by the giddiness of commutations.

JB: Our anti-destiny is the media universe. And I don't see how to make this mental leap which would make it possible to reach the fractal or fatal zones where things would really be happening. Collectively we are behind the radio-active screen of information. It is no more possible to go behind that curtain than it is to leap over your own shadow.

SL: You are one of the few thinkers to confront the gorgon of the media from within, to extract from it a vision — at the risk of being paralyzed. Yet you, too, need an advereary to succumb to your own fascination. And that partner can't be the media since you are yourself behind the screen; nor can it be reality, which you have left far behind. That partner is theory. Cultivating paradox in order to revulse theory, to upset its vision, to bring it to a crisis by playing and displaying the card of its own seriousness. That, I believe, is what your pleasure is, the only one maybe, or the only socializable one, at any rate a pleasure that is as strong as fascination.

JB: I admit that I greatly enjoy provoking that revulsion. But right away people ask, "What can you do with that?" It relies after all on an extraordinary deception — in the literal sense of the term. There is nothing to be had from it.

Paris — Rome, 1984-85

Notes

1. Elias Canetti, *The Human Province*, (New York: Seabury, 1978).

2. Jean Baudrillard, *The Mirror of Production*, (New York: Telos, 1975).

3. Jean Baudrillard, *Simulations*, (New York: Semiotext(e) Foreign Agents Series, 1983).

4. Gilles Deleuze, Felix Guattari, *Anti-Oedipus: Capitalism and Schizophrenia*, (New York: Viking, 1977).

5. In *Mille Plateaux*, (Paris: Editions de Minuit, 1980). See also *Nomadology: The War Machine* (New York: Semiotext(e) Foreign Agents Series, 1986).

6. Paul Virilio, *Speed and Politics*, (New York: Semiotext(e) Foreign Agents Series, 1986).

7. Georges Bataille, *La Part Maudite*, (Paris: Minuit, 1967). The "devil's share" is the portion of one's goods that cannot be spent usefully, but which must be offered sacrificially.

8. Jean Baudrillard, *In the Shadow of the Silent Majorities*, (New York: Semiotext(e) Foreign Agents Series, 1983).

9. ibid. "The End of the Social" comprises the second part.

10. ibid.

11. Jacques Monod, *Chance and Necessity*, (New York: Vintage, 1972).

12. Gilles Deleuze. *Logique du Sens*, (Paris: Minuit, 1969).

13. Jean Baudrillard, *De la Seduction*, (Paris: Galilee, 1979).

14. *Loving Boys*, (New York: Semiotext(e), 1980).

15. Paul Virilio, *L'Esthetique de la Disparition*, (Paris: Balland, 1980).

16. Paul Virilio/Sylvere Lotringer, *Pure War*, (New York: Semiotext(e) Foreign Agents Series, 1983).

17. Sophie Calle, *Suite Venitienne*, (Paris: Editions de l'Etoile, 1983).

18. *Autonomia: Post-Political Politics*, (New York: Semiotext(e), #9, 1980).

19 Jean Baudrillard, *Simulacres et Simulation*, (Paris: Galilee, 1981).

Translated by Phil Beitchman,
Lee Hildreth and Mark Polizzotti

Additional Semiotext(e) / Autonomedia Titles

SEMIOTEXT(E) USA
Jim Fleming & Peter Lamborn Wilson, Eds.
Designed by Sue Ann Harkey

A huge compendium of works in American
psychotopography. Anarchists, unidentifed flying
leftists, neo-pagans, secessionists, the lunatic fringe
of survivalism, cults, foreign agents, mad bombers,
ban-the-bombers, nudists, monarchists, chidren's
liberationsists, zero-workers, tax resisters, mimeo
poets, vampires, xerox pirates, pataphysicians,
witches, unrepentant faggots, hardcore youth, poetic
terrorists... The best of American *samizdat*.
Now available — $12 postpaid

SOVIETEXT[E]
Nancy Condee & Vladimir Padunov, Editors

Contemporary Soviet writers and artists and their
American critics contribute to an autonomous
examination of that country's newly-revolutionary
recent cultural and political transformations,
presenting material well beyond the sedate,
customary, officially approved networks of either
Russian or Western officialdom.
Summer, 1990 — $12 postpaid

Additional Semiotext(e) / Autonomedia Titles

ZERO GRAVITY
(*L'espace Critique*)
Paul Virilio

From the policing of ghettoes to defense satellites, from the politics of architecture to the conceptual technologies of space-time, from urban nomadism to post-modernism, cinema and the aesthetics of topologies, railroads and almanacs. By the author of *Speed and Politics* and *Pure War*.

Fall, 1990 — $12 postpaid

OVEREXPOSED
Treating Sexual Perversion in America
Sylvère Lotringer

An examination of "satiation therapy" in the treatment of sexual perversion in the United States, where sex offenders are "cured" by a form of behavior modification that consists of total immersion in the sexualized material that was formerly prohibited, by "boring their desire to death." A witty, sardonic account from the General Editor of *Semiotext(e)*.

A Pantheon Book.

Now Available — $12 postpaid